nailed it!

THE NAIL SALON CHRONICLES

nailed it!

THE NAIL SALON CHRONICLES

N. A. BANDA

VICKI H. MOSS

GRACE

BROKEN ARROW, OK

Cover Design: Yocla Designs

nailed it! THE NAIL SALON CHRONICLES

ISBN: 978-1-60495-039-7

DEDICATION

I would like to dedicate this book to my Savior, Jesus, for all He has done in me and how He took my little manicuring station and turned it into a work of the heart. He has blessed me with all of the words in this book as well as led me to pour into teen moms through Young Lives. And to my husband and three amazing, beautiful daughters who have always been encouraging and 100% supportive in all God has called me to, I am beyond grateful to do this adventure called life with them all.

~N.A. Banda

To PaPa and Cee Cee who enjoy discussing faith and Godcidents at their dining room table along with children and grandchildren — Hayden and Harper. (Hope, you were there in Mommie's womb and during the week; Mom and Dad had a baby reveal with cupcakes full of secrets. I'd already dreamed three times you were going to be a girl!) And a special thanks to Cee Cee for a grandmothers' day out with two darling grandies to enjoy a mani and pedi. If it weren't for Cee Cee I wouldn't have met Natalie that day in October 2016 at her manicure station. And she wouldn't have sent me her stories, and I wouldn't have been blessed to be a part of this book. God, indeed, works in mysterious ways to bring His children together.

~Vicki H. Moss

TABLE OF CONTENTS

FOREWORD

Not to brag, but I claimed an "A" in college statistics. So I knew the chances of a lifelong Tennessean — who rarely traveled to California — meeting Natalie Banda (a Cali girl) were slim to none.

When I travel, I enjoy a manicure and pedicure before my trip. Or I paint my own pigs, the name my grandchildren have labeled toes. Spending time in a nail salon while traveling is not how I envision spending my time while out of town, narrowing even more my chances of meeting Natalie. But meet her I did and the rest is history as they say. A totally divine appointment. She sent me her stories. And I discovered that Natalie is one of those people God provides for every generation, a person who asks the age old questions — Is it possible to connect with God in this day and age? Does prayer work? Why does God allow evil since He has the power to destroy it? Does God heal today when medicine fails? Does God guide His people when they ask? — and finds answers through Godcidents and longs for others to know they can connect with God as well.

Natalie's not the first to discover this truth. Mary Astor was a woman of her time who enjoyed vocational and material success amid movie stardom magic. She had it all: an academy award, incredible Beverly Hills mansions, jewelry and furs, children and star-struck marriages. But something was missing in her life. She admitted in print that "for years — even in the midst of fame and glamour — I yearned for contentment, happiness. It took me almost twenty years to go from idle curiosity about religion...to meeting God as a Person and a Father, and knowing that walking in faith meant growing up."

Natalie Banda is the mother of beautiful children and she has an incredible husband, but she's never won an academy award. She cannot boast about having similar Mary Astor successes when it comes to money and fame. Yet, she can boast about having a similar yearning for a close relationship with God that is worth more than mansions, jewelry and furs.

If you yearn for that closeness with God and wonder how to go about having a closer relationship with Him too, then this book is for you. Especially if you're ready to grow in amazing ways.

Vicki H. Moss

CHAPTER 1

HOW IT ALL BEGAN

I'm Natalie, an ordinary California manicurist with extraordinary appointments. My amazing call from God started when I was listening to a Christian radio station while driving to work one day. A song I loved was on — "The Power of Your Name" by Lincoln Brewster — and as I was singing, the words jumped into my heart and I began to pray.

I prayed with all I had in me and all of my heart, "Jesus, I want to be your hands and feet in this world, in whatever way you wish to use me."

That following month, I decided to run an online coupon for nail services. Within two days I sold a whopping 500 coupons.

Wow! What have I gotten myself into and how is this going to work?

Deciding to add Mondays to my schedule to fit everyone in, I managed with flying colors. What began to happen next has been happening for several years now. A Jesus trip for sure. I like to call these stories my *Nail Salon Chronicles*.

But where to begin? Meg's story is a good starting place. One of my first coupon moments began when a young girl sashayed into the salon. I can't recall her name or the conversation, but I did share a Godcident with her. After I'd finished she told me she was an atheist. But the story I told was a cool story, and I was excited to share with her. I said, "Hey, can I steal ten more minutes of your time to share one more testimony with you?" She agreed.

Right after I'd finished with this young girl's manicure, in strolled Meg. She sat down and as I was filing her nails, I couldn't hold back my excitement. I told her I'd just been able to share Jesus with a young girl who was an atheist. I was thrilled. And I can imagine this woman was probably thinking, *What kind of salon am I in?* Ha-ha!

While I literally held her "in the palm of my hands," I filed away and I shared this: "In 2009, my husband lost his job. We lost our home. The time was crazy though, because we had been attending church regularly for about three years. And in that three-year-period, something was happening. I couldn't put my finger on it. But something was sure happening. I felt like I should have been stressed, worried, and strung out. But I wasn't. I was at peace in the turmoil and through it all. Deep down, I felt that God was involved and was going to take care of us. With no more than two weeks to move and nowhere in sight to go and no money to go with, we walked out of our church on a Sunday, contemplating our dilemma.

"My husband looked over and said, 'We need to get back the money we loaned your parents when they moved.' I responded with: 'Were you just in the same church as I was — because I am pretty sure God just said He is going to provide.' I know. What boldness and sass. My husband looked over at me and said, 'Well, you must have more faith than I do.'

"So here's what happened next: I scheduled an appointment to view an apartment in a neighboring city and a townhome in our city. I desperately wanted the townhome so my girls could stay at their school. So, I did some hard praying. That week on Wednesday, as I was driving home from work, I received a text from my husband. 'Your prayers have been answered!' I assumed he was talking about the rental and their reply being a wonderful YES! Next, I began chatting with Jesus. 'Lord, where are we going to get the $5,000 needed to move in?' When I arrived home, I said, 'Great. The rental lady said *yes* to us, right?'

"My husband said, 'What lady?' Then he handed me a letter. 'Read this.' In my hand was a letter from a lawyer who represented the owners of my husband's previous place of employment. Ten years had passed since he'd worked for this company. The letter simply stated that if we signed and returned the attachment within seven days, we would receive a check for payment of such and such hours, or we could go to court for blank hours.

No dollar amount was mentioned. The completed attachment flew off in the mail the very next day.

"Then Saturday arrived and the phone call with, 'Yes, you've been chosen for the townhome.' Excited beyond belief, my next thought was, *Where is this money going to come from?*

"Monday rolled around and after picking up the kiddos I pulled into the driveway and grabbed the mail. Can you believe — if not, it's my truth — it just so happened we received a check from the law office of my husband's previous employer. A check for $5,000 (after taxes) and some change.

"God had nailed it — what an answer to my prayer! Almost to the penny, the money was what we needed for our move."

Sharing this story as I worked on Meg's nails, I looked up to see her in tears. "I've recently been afraid of losing my house, and now you tell me this," she told me.

Meg became a regular client and each week we were in awe of what God was doing at my little nail salon station.

After I had done her nails for a while, our friendship evolved outside of the salon. One night I received a text from her asking if I would go with her to be baptized.

My reply: YES!

Then she wrote that she wanted to get baptized in Puerto Rico. Yep. Puerto Rico. I had thought a local church would be pretty cool. I was speechless. But the funny thing is, being a Puerto Rican is a big part of my ethnicity and I'd never been to Puerto Rico. I replied with, "Let me run this by my husband real quick ha-ha-ha!" So off we flew for a baptism in Puerto Rico. Way out of my comfort zone because I hated flying. And there we were flying off a continent to an itty bitty island. Who would have thought that God would use an online coupon to take me across a continent and an ocean to such a beautiful place?

Could it be that God turned a little nail station into a bubbling fountain filled with Godcidents? I believed so.

The stories were endless…not just me sharing, but others sharing as well, by way of one connecting word.

Now, I cannot wait for you to read about other stories. But for the moment, let me share something a client told me that will probably be my favorite quote from now on.

My overbooked coworker had asked me to take a client. In she walked at 5:30 p.m. She usually had her toes done by my coworker but since my co-worker was unavailable, I greeted her. In conversation, she said, "I like your look." I appreciated the compliment. She then asked about my kids and what my husband did for a living. I replied, "Funny you should ask that. He just got fired on Monday."

"I'm so sorry," the woman replied.

"Don't be," I said. "You see, I serve a mighty God

who had already set up another job the same day." That opened our conversation to sharing our faith and love for Jesus. Then she said this — the line I love — "At church, you know what you're getting…who's there, etc. But then there's this farmers market in a nail salon where the food is organic, true and good."

For me that was an even better compliment than her liking my look! I knew I'd be using her line from then on. But truly, the glory and praise she showered on me belongs to "He who is in me."

That story gets even better with the telling. I shared the same story with my co-writer, Vicki Moss, but I'll let her share what happened during her visit to my nail bar.

Hailing from Tennessee, I had no real desire to fly across the country to California. My daughter, Peyton, had moved back home from San Francisco via a stint in Denver, Colorado and I doubted I'd ever have a need to go back to the West Coast. Airfare was sky high — pardon the pun — and flying with all of the rules and regulations has made traveling a downright nuisance. Dealing with airport security can sometimes be a royal pain.

But when Peyton and her husband, Chris, asked me to keep my grandies so they could attend a family wedding in California, his parents were disappointed the children weren't flying out with them. They suggested I come too and keep the children at their house while they joined the wedding party for a couple of days. The rest of the trip, we'd spend free hours together.

Since the other grandparents didn't get to see the grandchildren as often as I did, I agreed to babysit in Papa's and Cee Cee's home. Plus, we'd all be together for a new grandie baby reveal which would be fun. So off I flew with the kids and grandies for an adventure in a small town about an hour from San Francisco.

During dinner one night, the subject of religion came up — with everyone expressing their opinions and beliefs. I shared a pretty far out tale about an incident that had happened to me, and in the telling I acknowledged that it was difficult for some to believe that Jesus is still alive and well, still working miracles today, and if believers desire, they can have a close relationship with God. My eldest granddaughter, five-year-old Hayden, turned to me and with the belief that only an innocent child can have, she said, "Lovie, I believe you!"

I could only imagine that the angels in heaven were rejoicing at this simple, yet beautiful confession of faith from this little child who believed my story was true. And if my story was true, then what the Bible said about Jesus is also indeed true. He was born to be nailed to a cross making it possible for humanity to be saved from sin through the shedding of his blood.

I'd been reading Bible stories with my grandies since they were tiny and had been teaching them John 14:6:

Jesus told him, "I am the way, the truth, and the life. No one can come to the Father except through me." We'd talked about God's creation, angels, and the coming of the Christ child, baby Jesus — Savior of mankind. And we'd worshipped together in the same church singing and praising the awe-inspiring God of the universe.

To hear this child say with such enthusiasm and passion, "Lovie, I believe you!" meant so much and warmed my heart. What a priceless moment!

The next day, both grandmothers were taking our granddaughters for a pedicure-and-manicure outing. Living with expectancy, I prayed on the way to the nail salon that something wonderful might happen while we were out. Praying that we might meet someone special, I was seeking a God-moment for us all. Something that might show that God and Jesus are real and they still speak to us today if we're open to what they have to say.

We walked into the nail salon and Hayden and I were assigned to Natalie. She was professional and all smiles, so I knew the experience would be a good one. I just wasn't prepared for how good. Deliciously good. In our conversation, Natalie said something about Young Life. "So you're a Christian then?"

"Of course," replied Natalie with the brightest smile. I could tell she was filled with the Holy Spirit. Her countenance glowed with an irrepressible light that shone from deep within.

"Would you share one of your stories with us," I asked, praying it would be a story that would impress two little girls with feet warming in water in preparation for getting their "pigs" painted.

And share Natalie most certainly did. She told the story about how God provided the $5,000 for her move to a new place. My grandies' eyes were about to pop out of their little heads as they listened. In some ways, Natalie reminded me of a devout Christian by the name of George Muller — a man who lived in England in the 1800's. Muller set out to prove to his church members that God still provided, as He was the same God yesterday, today, and tomorrow. In doing so, he prayed to start orphanages that would be sustained by prayer for the needs of the children. Through prayer, George depended on God and God alone to move people to send money, clothing, and food for the daily needs of his charges.

Imagine my surprise when six months later, I received an email with Natalie's stories. I was enthralled. I'd found a kindred spirit who also believed that through prayer, God still does amazing things. And I'm not talking about prosperity preaching involving gimmee-gimmee type prayers. Jesus said the poor will always be with us so not all will be wealthy, though provision for "needs" are promised if one believes.

Natalie believes, as I do, that if you first seek the kingdom of God, all else will be added unto you. We might not all be rich, but as believers we know God promises to supply needs for those willing to ask. Needs and wants are two different things.

And our prayers are supposed to be prayers not only asking for material things needed or desired, but prayers of thanksgiving, prayers of intercession on behalf of others, prayers of faith, and prayers of consecration. I later learned that Natalie, like me, had some pretty amazing stories and had experienced some crazy wild happenings while being a servant of God. I mean, who ever thought God would work through coupons? But during the pedicure, I laughed and teared up at one of the stories she shared with us. Mostly, I rejoiced! It was wonderful to know that God had been busy in California as well as in Tennessee.

But enough about me. Read Natalie's take on our meeting.

When Vicki came in with the other grandmother and their two grandchildren, I was assigned to one of the girls. While doing her mani and chatting with Vicki, due to Vicki's accent I asked where she was from. She told me Tennessee and I said, "A good friend of mine and my daughter's moved there and they love it. We knew them through Young Life." Vicki said, "I know about Young Life. My kids participated."

When we moved to the pedicure area, I shared a

story with them. Before they left I shared how I had been in the back folding towels and praying for clients, then I came out and in they walked. Before they left Vicki said, "We should keep in touch." I asked if she was active on Instagram and gave her my Instagram page. That night when I was home, Vicki sent me a private message sharing how she had prayed that morning that God would show Himself the next day on their outing to a nail salon. I then went to Vicki's Instagram gallery and saw she was a writer. I told her how I'd tried to write something a few years ago and asked if maybe she would be interested in seeing what I'd written.

And as they say, the rest is history.

CHAPTER 2

Conviction and Humility

For the next divine appointment, how about Lola? Lola walked in with her coupon and immediately I judged her. I remember thinking she was a snob from an area close to us — neighborhoods filled with many wealthy people.

God loves to show me through different ways and means and in the process, humble me. But I know it's because He loves me and wants me to keep growing.

But back to Lola. At my station sat a little lamp and on it was a tiny paper with a recorded scripture. Psalm 51:10: *Create in me a clean heart....* Go figure. At that moment my mindset was not very clean. Guess I was really asking for it.

Lola looked at the lamp and said, "That is one of my favorite verses." Yep. There it was. Conviction and humility ran through me. God must have arranged our meeting to "nail" my judgmental self to the wall. He nailed it alright.

Lola shared how during the previous year she had lived the life of Job. If you don't know the story of Job I encourage you to read it. The short version is that God gave the devil the go-ahead to attack Job in every way as long as he didn't kill him. But Job was a man of patience and perseverance. After losing all of his children and his livestock, even his wife told him to curse God and die. But Job refused to turn his back on God. And now Lola was telling me she'd lived the life of Job?

She said she'd lost a few family members; one cousin was the only fatality in a huge multi-car pileup. Then this: "I never worked. My husband was the breadwinner and we adopted two children. After being married for years and attending church — my husband even served at the church — one day close to Easter, he walked in and said, 'I'm leaving.' I thought he was going to the store so I said, 'Can you bring home some milk?'

"He said, 'No. I am leaving you for someone else.'"

Yep. Heartbreak crazy. Not only did her husband leave her, he hid all of their money in another bank account. She was alone, felt destitute, and it seemed she had nothing. But one thing she did have...God. The church she attended kept its doors open for 24 hours during the celebration of the risen Christ. "I would go at three A.M. and sit to read, cry, and pray. Amazingly, the people at the church began to step up and help me. One time while sitting there weeping and praying, a woman who worked at the church approached and handed me an envelope with my name written on it. She said it had been left under her door. Inside I found money and a note to see a certain counselor."

Lola's grief was palpable. While she was re-living all of this sadness and the heartbreak of being alone, I said, "Hey, was the counselor's name so and so?" And she said, "Yes, how did you know that?"

"I used to do her nails in that town years ago. I know she is an amazing counselor and loves Jesus!"

Only then did the laughter bubble up so Lola could continue her story. "I began trusting in God and asked Him to lead me. I opened my own yoga studio and have traveled the world as an instructor."

On her way out that day, Lola paused, and turned to say, "My favorite verse is Joshua 1:9: *This is my command – be strong and courageous! Do not be afraid, or discouraged. For the Lord your God is with you wherever you go.*"

Do you know, the very next day I was in a Christian bookstore and at the checkout saw a name card. It had one of my client's names on it and the verse for her name was Joshua 1:9. Okay, then! So the next day I drove to the mall because it was my anniversary that weekend and I wanted this eye shadow I had seen on Pinterest. A super cute girl was helping me at the Mac counter when I noticed she sported a tattoo on her wrist. I asked her if I could see it and as she turned her wrist toward me, there it was again. Joshua 1:9.

I'd always heard that God talks to us through His

Word and oftentimes, if He is directly trying to tell us something, it comes our way three times. That next day, in Napa Valley while wine tasting and contemplating what wine will be served when Jesus marries His church — red, white, or blush *wink,* you know the selection will be a good one because He'll be making that wine himself — I told my husband about hearing and seeing Joshua 1:9 everywhere of late. I told him, "Let's look up that verse to see exactly what it says." The next Monday, I sat at my kitchen table writing this very story in my journal. The thing is, I'd had this journal for quite some time and never once noticed until that day that on the cover of my journal were the same words and scripture verse…Joshua 1:9.

It was and still is my belief that the very same God who created the heavens and earth was speaking directly to me. Over and over and over, again and again — He continues every day if you simply pay attention and listen.

Jeremiah 29:13 tells us the Lord said, *"If you look for me wholeheartedly, you will find me."*

Not only do I believe it, Vicki believes it. She shares a story of her own about God's way of grabbing our attention. Three times no less!

I've noticed there's something about the number three that God loves. There's the Trinity: God, Jesus, and the Holy Ghost. Gideon approached God three times and put out the fleece to make sure God was talking to him. Jesus rose from the grave in three days. Peter denied Christ three times. There are many more examples too numerous to mention.

I once heard Jill Briscoe, an evangelist speaker, share with her audience how she'd tried to launch a neighborhood Bible study when living in London. The Lord told her to go out and canvass the neighborhood while strolling her child, and ask all of the women to come to her Bible study one night during the week.

She cooked and baked all day and when the night arrived, not one woman showed her face. Jill cried and went back to God and said, "Lord, I did what you told me to do and no one showed." The Lord said, "Go back and ask again." Trying to be obedient, Jill ventured out a second time and asked everyone again. This time, some were so embarrassed that they'd told her they would come and didn't —hoping the other neighbors would go — that they said they would come the next time. One blind woman stated she didn't get out after dark. Jill thought that odd, but plodded on to the next house. And to the next. And the next. One door opened to reveal a deaf woman and Jill shouted her invitation, not knowing if she'd been heard.

She trudged back home and as the Bible-study day arrived, she baked and cooked all over again. Still no one showed. She cried, and ventured back to God in prayer.

He told her to go out a third time. She slung some more tears and said, "God, I can't go a third time!" God was relentless. He told her to go, so she gathered her wounded pride and fluffed up her courage to troop out a third time.

That night, two women showed up for her Bible study...the deaf woman was leading the blind woman. "Great!" Jill thought to herself. "One can't read the scripture and the other can't hear it!"

What mattered was that she was obedient, and finally, she did make headway with the two women. They seemed to be *getting the gospel.* She shouted it from the rooftops to the one and tried to give a clear visual picture to the other. Eventually, her home ministry blossomed into a gathering of eighty women.

I heard Jill tell that story and reasoned that I would have loved to have had someone invite me into their home when I was a young mother, to be fed physically as well as spiritually, and not have to bring food or wash a dish.

After I'd volunteered at Precept Ministries to learn how to teach one of Kay Arthur's 40-minute Bible studies, I decided to do something similar to what Jill Briscoe had done. Maybe the women wouldn't mind me teaching them if I plied them with good food.

Soup and salad. That's what I'd prepare!

Easy and quick, using fine china, my best silverware, and crystal. Make them feel like queens.

Then fear crept in. Not a valiant warrior, I worried. What if no one showed? My family would be eating soup until the next week! I invited ten people and paced the kitchen floor close to the window, watching and waiting, terrified no one would come.

With tears, I trudged back to God pleading in prayer, "Lord, I'm not Jill Briscoe. You have one shot at getting me to do this. Someone had better show the first time because I don't have the faith Jill Briscoe has to ask again."

I wasn't married to a preacher either and Jill Briscoe was, like that really mattered to God. And I truly figured she had more faith than I did. More than likely, I was probably from the same gene pool as Doubting Thomas most of the time.

As I watched the clock and fretted, finally, seven women wheeled into my driveway, driving chariots of fire and right on time. God had heard and answered my prayers. I wiped my eyes and washed up odd dishes at the kitchen sink, thankful for my angels of mercy.

I planned on a forty-minute study, getting the women out of there within the hour so those who were pressed for time could get back to work. One young woman was a teacher; the principal of her school allowed her to come to the study because he was also a Christian. Another woman was an attorney; she scheduled her court cases around the study. One lady grew up in the denomination of her brothers but had converted to a different Christian denomination when she married. Because she was employed by her brothers, to get time off during office hours, she told them she needed to attend a *meeting* rather than a Bible study, otherwise they wouldn't have excused her to attend a function that wasn't of their denomination.

For some, what initially was to be a one-hour study turned into two hours. We hashed and rehashed scriptural truths and had a wonderful time doing so. One attendee dropped out but I never had less than five.

I prepared a different soup every week and arranged fresh flowers on the table to brighten everyone's lunchtime. When my front door opened, their nostrils were assailed with smells of comfort. Soup, salad, and bread that were left over after supper could be taken to shut-ins. I photocopied the recipes I used for each lunch day and left them on the table for those who wished to try the soup and bread recipes later for their families. Kay Arthur was gracious enough to send me her favorite soup recipe. Preparing it one week, I was delighted to be able to pass it on to *my* ladies.

I wrote a letter to Kay, just in case I couldn't make it to an update meeting, to let her know how my class was going. Somehow I knew I wasn't going to make the scheduled meeting. Holy Spirit? Sure enough, Kay had to change the meeting date and I wasn't available to keep the appointment for the new date. I was glad I'd already written out the letter for Kay to be delivered via email through my Precept leader, Jan Priddy.

I then received an email from Jan that read, "Vicki, your email was so encouraging that I forwarded part of it to Kay. She has used your inviting people in for Bible study and lunch with the 40 minute studies as an example for women around the world...."

Later, I again heard from Jan. Kay had read a portion of the letter at the meeting I'd missed and had said, "Now this, ladies, is the way to teach a Bible study!" Jan also wrote, "She (Kay) asked me to send it [her response] to you, and she wants to meet you, so on Tuesday morning after her lecture, please come down front, so I can introduce the two of you." The response from Kay read: "Vicki dear...Jan shared your email and my heart is full of rejoicing. Thank you for your sensitive heart to the Holy Spirit...your listening ear, your obedience. I rejoice! Much love, Kay." This was wonderful encouragement and I continued with the ladies attending my Soup and Salad Bible study.

Not only was the study uplifting for the others and me, my daughter Peyton walked in smiling one day and said, "You know Mom, I love coming home from school to fresh flowers every Wednesday, knowing the house is going to smell like some new yummy soup."

Her favorite recipe was my very own *Get Lucky Soup*.

That's the one where I threw all of the refrigerator leftovers like chicken, potatoes, and carrots into a rich creamy milk laced with butter — sort of my gourmet signature soup with added onions. (The recipe's at the end of the book.)

When shopping for the ingredients for my recipes and purchasing fresh flowers at the grocery, I lingered around exotic orchids before moving on to select roses. Every time, I thought, *I would love to have an orchid but they are so expensive and I don't have the green thumb for indoor plants,* and I reluctantly passed them by.

Warm weather teasing the air, one night I thumbed through a Springhill Nursery catalog I'd received in the mail. Stopping at one page I thought, "*Mmmmm, lilac bush. I don't have a lilac bush in my garden. I need to purchase one.*" I kept my dream flowers to myself thinking maybe one day, I might splurge and dig a hole for my heart's desire.

I went on to other Southern reading material where I read, "Watch out when it says 'lo and berhol' in the Bible 'cause the Lawd's getting ready to do something big."

Well, *lo and berhol,* on the last day of class, one lady showed up with a lilac bush for my garden and two others strolled in with an exquisite white orchid. Another brought a beautiful silver prayer necklace. No one knew that I'd been secretly wishing for the plants because I hadn't spoken my desires to a soul. The necklace was a bonus. I was stunned and speechless. Three gifts! I hadn't expected a thing except making it to the end of that class with people still attending and me still standing!

After God had enlarged my territory as he did for Jabez in I Chronicles, He'd blessed me indeed and I was still amazed over those two particular gifts; gifts God knew I'd wanted though I'd never verbalized my wishes. I'd never expected a thing in return for what I was doing. I was only trying to bless God, Kay, and others.

When I first sought the kingdom of God and was obedient, God loved favoring me with a double portion (like he did Job for all his trouble) and then delighting me with something He knew I would enjoy.

Now that my faith has grown, who knows — I might go for three tries wth the next Bible study, if I'm rejected and no one shows the first time.

Faith as strong as Kay Arthur's and Jill Briscoe's, and a relationship with God are something that is planted, watered and harvested. Like a seed, they simply grow. And *Lo and Berhol* — I think there is just something about God and the number three!

And this story gets even better. Later, when trying to recall the details about the correspondence with Jan Priddy regarding my notes on my Soup and Salad Bible Study class and trying to edit this book for publication, my house sold. I was in for a move during Christmas holidays. Arrggggh! And since I was in the middle of a move, I had to put this book on hold.

Almost four months later as I was opening boxes in my new home, I came across some old folders with manuscripts. Thumbing through the folders, I found copies of the emails from Jan Priddy and Kay Arthur that verified my story, and I could quote from the emails verbatim. I had placed copies of the emails with a hard copy of "God and the Number Three" in the folder back in 2005. What were the odds that I would open that particular box — one out of a hundred boxes yet to be opened — and why in the world did I go through those folders one by one to discover emails I didn't recall receiving? Procrastinating on editing, maybe? For sure!

But I think there's more to the story. Evidently, God's timing for *nailed it* to be published was not mine and Natalie's timing. Only His. Plus, I needed time away from the manuscript before going back to look at it with fresh and rested eyes and God wanted me to find those emails to give more validation to my story. He provided me with backup!

CHAPTER 3

TEACHABLE MOMENTS

Who should be next....

How about Asha? Her story is one you'll want to hear.

So, in walked Asha with her coupon and she settled into the pedicure chair. As I was filling up the pedi bowl with warm water she said, "I like your cross bracelet."

"Thank you," I replied. She then asked if she could listen to her headphones and I said, "Of course. It's your time." I started her service by taking off old polish. She looked down and said, "Ohhhh, do you have crosses on your nails too?"

"Yes, I do," I replied. "I love Jesus because He is so great." Her response? "Yes. He is." And without batting an eyelash she added, "I just met Him in February of this year at Disneyland."

Yep. That was her answer.

My reply? "You know, I go there all the time and I never see him." Then off came the headphones and her story spilled out like water tumbling over boulders. "I was born in India and raised Hindu my entire life. When I was of marriageable age, I married someone from my same country but with more strict ideas. We had children. We then moved to California and my new story was about to begin. We'd bought a house and it was just after the Christmas holidays. The real estate agent dropped by with a gift basket for us — his new homeowners. I began to tell him how I now wanted to sell the house. For some strange reason, I opened up to this real estate agent about my — by then — abusive husband and how I wanted a divorce. This realtor was from India as well but was a Christian. He began to tell me that I should forgive my husband instead of carrying around all of this hate. I didn't understand what he was talking about and instead grew more miserable. As February was approaching, I decided life was no longer worth living.

"I'd planned a trip to Disneyland as a last trip. After that I would come home and take my life. The night I packed for Mom and the kids, readying them for the trip, I couldn't sleep. I kept thinking of the realtor and what He had said. I decided I needed a Bible and searched for a nearby store where I could quickly drive to purchase a Bible. Not finding a store open, I found a Bible app on my phone. The words began with "*In the beginning....*" I listened all night and during the entire drive down to Disneyland.

"It must have been God's doing because my kids didn't bother me during the entire drive — which was totally unlikely. If you have children, you know what I mean. After arriving at the hotel, I called the realtor and began to tell him that he was right about forgiveness and right about the hate I was holding inside.

"He asked, 'What has prompted your call?' I replied, 'I've been listening to the Bible on my trip to Disneyland.' He said, 'Where did you start?'

"'The beginning, of course.'

"He said, 'Well, skip to the New Testament. It's where we live today. You can always go back and read the Old Testament.' That day, I listened to Matthew, Mark, and Luke in the lines at Disney. It so happened that I stood there in a slow moving line, and this God looked down and saw me. He not only saw, He reached down, and saved my life in Disneyland."

Hard to believe I know, right there in front of Mickey, Minnie, and Pluto and hordes of people ga-ga over Cinderella, Snow White, and Goofy. Or while moving an inch or two every now and then to finally pay for a foot-long dog and soft drink at the burger stand. To meet Jesus in such a place!

I was speechless hearing this fantastical story. Plus it made me want a vacation at Disney. Especially if Jesus could be found there!

Fast forward a year almost to the day. I ran another online coupon and in walked Asha again. Distraught. After her trip to Disneyland, God had asked her to stay in her bad marriage. As I filed her nails, she said,

"Natalie, I am verbally abused, banned from owning a Bible, much less reading one, and so I have to sneak to Bible study. Neighbors from the same culture as I'm from have come over to tell me I am a disgrace to my family. So much persecution, yet Jesus told me to stay."

Asha came back only a handful of times as she managed to sneak away, and we fellowshipped together. It was so hard for me to understand her staying with this abusive husband even though she knew it was God's will for her.

Then a long time passed without seeing or hearing from her until one day in came an email from Asha, inviting me to her baptism. I immediately called her and asked her to come in. When she arrived, the next part of her story began to unfold.

"One night after being faithful and enduring, God told me I could be set free. I walked downstairs to find divorce papers and my parents had agreed to help me. My husband left and I went outside and wept. Loud, deep-down weeping. There was a hillside in my backyard. I heard Jesus say, 'Look up.' There before me was a row of angels. I knew then I had never been alone.

"In the Bible it says the pure of heart shall see God. I am human and flawed and sin but my heart is so pure for God. I wanted to obey. I wanted only what God wanted and He gave me a glimpse into how He was protecting me and how he was always near. Soon my one prayer was that my family would receive Jesus, and one by one my prayers began to be answered as they saw what He had done and what He was doing in my life."

After hearing Asha's story, I realized that in a short hour of work, I had experienced something no one could probably imagine happening in a little nail salon.

These Godcidents aren't just for me. God works around the world for those who are open to His guidance. Anyone can make incredible connections during a time of need or a time of sharing. God can arrange for meetings with people you're supposed to meet for whatever the reason may be whether it's at work, at the mall, or on vacation. God connects His people with others, depending on what needs are.

Vicki was even able to minister to a taxi driver.

For once in my life, I was keeping my mouth shut. Usually, after hailing a cab I chat nonstop, picking the driver's brain for information. But today, I wanted to enjoy quiet time because the high altitude had been causing a problem with my head all week and now with another headache coming on I didn't feel that great.

"On vacation?" The guy sounded like a magpie. "Have a good time? Visiting family or friends?"

"God," I muttered, "can I not have a little peace and quiet? My head hurts." The answer back from Him was a resounding, "No."

"Fine then. I'll talk about You, and these days, the mention of your name alone should silence him." So I said out loud, "What a beautiful day the Lord has made."

Looking into the rear view mirror, I saw raised eyebrows. "Christian?" Surprised he would go there, I nodded.

"I'm a Christian too. But you know, I've never learned how to talk to God. I don't know how to pray."

Before I could blurt out, *You're a Christian and you never learned how to pray?* I was suddenly reminded, *Praying publicly hasn't always been easy for you....*

True. And leave it to the Holy Spirit to be a counselor who gets to the heart of the matter in a heartbeat.

But now, what was basic to me was alien to this man. I explained, "Keep it simple. Talk to God like you would an earthly father who loves you. Thank Him for all He's done. Share with him about your life. Needs. Desires. Mention others who need help or healing. He knows everything before you say it or ask but go ahead and pour your heart out."

Then I shared about a book that had made an impact on my life: *The Prayer of Jabez.* In front of the airport terminal, I prayed with him before exiting the cab and prayed the prayer of Jabez over him. He held holy hands up and said, "I feel your prayers already! Hallelujah!"

After he retrieved my luggage, I hugged him goodbye and wished him well.

Elated from our conversation, he said, "I'll purchase the book, take it back home to Ethiopia in two weeks, then share with family and friends about the book and the woman who taught me to pray!"

I was reminded of Acts 8:29-31: *The Holy Spirit said to Philip, "Go over and walk along beside the carriage." Philip ran over and heard the man reading from the prophet Isaiah. Philip asked, "Do you understand what you are reading?" The man replied, "How can I, unless someone instructs me?" And he urged Philip to come up into the carriage and sit with him.*

God had arranged my "chariot" encounter!

What a lost teachable moment this would have been if I'd remained silent. I would have missed a chance to pray with an Ethiopian brother in Christ who needed guidance. I wouldn't have seen new light in hungry eyes or heard, "I feel your prayers already! Hallelujah!"

God sure nailed that chariot encounter.

CHAPTER 4

MODERN DAY MIRACLES

One night was so cool. And I'm not talking about the temperature. A mother, Dianna, and her daughter, Lee, were scheduled for pedicures. When they walked in, I noticed the mother radiated with such a joyful spirit. As I filled her pedicure tub I thought, *She must know Jesus.* Then a few moments later she said, "Natalie, do you know Jesus?" I was amazed and excited and replied, "Yes, I sure do."

Her daughter, Lee, laughed and said, "My Mom does this all the time."

I thought her boldness was great and I wanted to be bold like that and step up for Jesus and ask people if they knew Him. In the asking, a door can be opened to share Jesus with someone who has not encountered Him.

We had the best conversation. Dianna was so wise and shone with love for the Savior. To this day I am still Lee's manicurist and Dianna is an amazing voice of wisdom and truth in my life. There was a time when I had no place to work for a little while and Dianna offered the use of her home without charging me rent for a place where I could go to do nails. My heart was to do nails for women who could not afford the services, and to do it in such a way where they could be around the Spirit of God and receive nail services with any amount of donation they could make. When I arrived at Dianna's house the day we first started, I couldn't believe my eyes. The setting of her home was on a beautiful and serene mountain top.

I said, "Dianna, you already live in heaven. You are so blessed with this gorgeous home."

An amazing woman, Dianna said, "I asked God for this, to bless me and I would use my home for His work." After first seeking the Kingdom of God, she was blessed with an incredible place and now she does just what she said she would do — she serves Him through the use of her home.

Let me describe Dianna: She welcomes everyone, loves pouring visitors a cup of tea, and then enjoys sharing Jesus.

I'm also thankful for her daughter, Lee. She comes in for a manicure and gives me carte blanche to do whatever designs I want on her nails. I cherish those clients who let me indulge in my artistic creativity, and we have the best conversations about all of these stupendous God moments in our lives.

I firmly believe that God sometimes has people come in and out of our lives for a moment or a season. But He also blesses us with lifetime friends and those who are in our lives for fellowship, encouragement, and living life together. Dianna and Lee are friends of that special category. Though we don't see each other frequently, our connection with the Lord makes it seem as if no time has passed between visits. Love those ladies! And who would have ever known that I would be writing a book including their story? God knew but I would have never guessed. And it's truly amazing how God has woven our stories together. This story is for them and a tribute to all of their prayers and support during my walk and ministry with Young Lives — a ministry God has called me to.

There have been times when I really wanted someone to stay in my life, but life pulled them away. Or God simply removed them. Being without those special friends is hard at times, but I know His plan is perfect and for the best. So I've learned to trust His way and plan.

One night in October 2012 my husband and I watched a movie titled *Flywheel*. The husband in the movie was losing his job and their lives were falling apart. God was all they had to rely on. That same scenario would play out in my personal life a few days later.

My husband lost his job, as I'd previously mentioned, and we could no longer afford our townhome. For the month of November we borrowed the money for rent and I was able, for the first time, to pay all other bills. December came and circumstances worsened making it impossible to stay. We needed a miracle.

A Christmas miracle did take place that December. On Monday December 10th, I was driving and having a serious talk with Jesus. I prayed, "I know Christmas isn't about gifts, but Jesus, I love giving gifts at this time. Please provide a way for me to do so."

That Wednesday, some clients I have known for many years were scheduled for my services. As I approached their home, I was listening to a sermon in my car. I'll never forget the date — 12-12-12. As I cut the engine on my car, the preacher on the radio said, "The Lord put it on my heart that he was going to bless people today."

When I walked into my client's home, the mom pulled me aside and said, "I never really hear from God, but today I heard Him very clearly. You see, Natalie, each year my family and I gather money together to donate to a chosen cause or Christmas project. This year, God has told me to give the money to you and your family." I broke down in tears and told her that I'd just prayed for a miracle of this magnitude a few days before.

That following weekend my husband and I were driving one of our daughters to her sporting event in Las Vegas. On the drive there I shared with him about God's provision through my client. I was stunned when he told me that something similar had happened to him.

He said he'd also prayed that week for provision for a new suit for a job interview and money to afford the trip to Vegas for our daughter's event. My husband said,

"A friend of mine who never really talks about God messaged me. I met with him and he said he felt a strong prompting that day to give me an envelope with money."

Even though we knew we had to move New Year's Eve and didn't know what was coming next, I still felt so blessed to share both of these seemingly small — but large to us — miracles with my family on Christmas day.

God was showing up daily in my life and my mouth felt like it was stuck on repeat as I shared the stories with others. As each client wandered into the salon where I happened to be working, the stories about God — His grace and His mercy and provision — poured out of me like sweet honey.

Once, I said to my husband, "You know, it's bizarre. I can never pinpoint or clearly remember how these Jesus conversations get started."

Then one day I read this line in a devotional: "Do not offer the world your words or thoughts then offer them dry crumbs. Instead let my living water flow through you...." I came to believe that without a doubt, the Holy Spirit was initiating these wonderful conversations.

CHAPTER 5

God's Soft Voice

With my newfound and very lively relationship with Jesus came all kinds of out-of-my-comfort-zone episodes, including an amazing devotional book that popped into my life and salon.

One day, Christa, a dear friend of mine, invited me to a women's gathering that was being conducted that night. The event was taking place at another lady's home.

I was cautious about going to places where I knew no one. In addition, my schedule at work was booked up into the evening and to attend I would have to cancel some appointments to even make it. Still, in the middle of the day I kept feeling like God wanted me to cancel appointments and go. But there was a problem: One of my last clients was a regular who tipped extremely well. I knew that if I cancelled on her, more than likely, she would not return. Yet, I felt I had no choice but to cancel her appointment.

I was clearly hearing God's soft voice and nudging all day to go, so I obeyed. And yes, I never saw that coveted client again. But that's okay. Because the night spent with other women at the ladies event proved to be worth more than money. The woman who hosted was sharing about her life. When she was finished she held a devotional book in her hand. She said, "This devotional book — *Jesus Calling* by Sarah Young — changed my entire life and I want each of you to have one." After a wonderful evening with women who also loved the Lord, I left for home with my devotional book and memories of new friends. (After all of the books were passed out, I also met a remarkable woman named Lisa. I'll share some of her story later.)

Then, one day I was so upset about our living situation — the cost of living in California is very expensive — I felt like asking God, "Why are you punishing me?"

I strode into work and a regular client asked if I was okay. I replied, "No. And do you want to know why? The devil is attacking me today and he's winning! Ugh!"

I told her about my wonderful night at the ladies event and the book I'd received, which was conveniently tucked inside my purse. Eager for some relief, I grabbed the book and said, "Let's read today's devotional."

I'll never forget the message on that page. Something like, "The world is spinning around and everything is a blur. If you put Me in the center where We meet and do not look to the world for sustenance, etc...." I was given the message I so badly needed for that particular day and time. God had nailed it again. How could He have inspired Sarah Young to write that book knowing I would need that specific message on that particular day? Sarah had never met a woman named Natalie Banda and had no idea another woman would pass the devotional book on to me so I would turn to a specific page on a downbeat day. But God knew. He knows everything since He is omniscient.

Each time I read a devotional from the book, I was met with words that seemed perfect for what I was going through each day. And each time I read the book now, even though years have passed, the words are always relevant.

After that mind-blowing experience, there were even more cool experiences or Godcidents. One day, I drove in on a Sunday to meet a client. She started telling me how her marriage was a mess. She asked, "How are you always writing about Jesus and never seem to worry? I glanced at my station and *Jesus Calling*, the book I'd been given, was there. Placing the book in her hands, I said, "Take this book. Read it and pray and let God show you the way."

A few days later, at the end of her appointment another regular client said, "I almost forgot. One Sunday a woman was selling these books and I felt I should get you one."

Yep. You guessed it. The book she handed me was the same devotional book I'd recently given away. *Jesus Calling*. It goes without saying, but let me go ahead and say it — I was blown away. "This is nuts!" I exclaimed. "I just gave this same book away on Sunday!"

I have given that book away again and again, and it has been given back to me again and again. The little darling is like the best little book I can't keep but have to have.

God will provide a word whether it comes by word of mouth or in book form. Vicki has her own book story.

My daughter, Peyton, had totaled her car in a nasty car accident. Luckily she survived with no more than a few scratches. But then there was the car that needed to be replaced. So off we drove with the family — in my car — to the dealership to try and find a good deal on a used automobile. Once there, other family members decided they needed to trade, so while they were out combing the lot for a deal, I sat inside at the salesman's desk until I heard, "Mom, come out and take a look at this car and see what you think. It's used and in good shape."

I offered my opinion and returned to the salesman's desk. On the desk before me lay something that hadn't been there before. A book about Billy Sunday. When Peyton later walked in and sat down next to me, I picked the book up and said, "Look at this. A book titled *Billy Sunday — the Man and His Message*. I have been searching the internet for a copy of this book for months. There was not one to be found."

"Who is Billy Sunday?" Peyton asked.

"He was one of Billy Graham's mentors. I just finished Billy Graham's autobiography and Billy Sunday was mentioned a couple of times. And I'm wondering, *Who in the world is Billy Sunday?* So I started searching for this book. And I came up empty handed. I didn't see anyone put this book on this desk, did you? Where did it come from? Books don't just magically appear out of thin air. Especially religious books. In a car dealership."

"Mom, calm down."

"I'm not calming down. I'm going to get to the bottom of how this book got here!"

About that time, the young car salesman approached his desk. Holding up the book, I demanded, "Whose book is this?"

I must have had a wild, hungry look in my eyes — because I *was* wild and hungry for God and needed to know how other people experienced Him. The salesman cautiously replied, "It belongs to the used car manager."

"And what does he do with it at work?" I asked, on pins and needles now for an answer.

"Umm. He teaches out of it in morning meetings. Uses it sort of like a devotional book before we pray and hit the sales floor."

"Is that so?" I replied, not sure if I believed him. "You're telling me you pray before you sell cars?" Not waiting for an answer I said, "Tell him to come out here. I want to meet him." By this time Peyton was squirming in her seat, thinking her mother had lost it. But I would not be deterred. I was determined to get an answer. This was not some used car lot with a hovel of an office on a side road trying to sell used cars. This was one of the largest dealerships in town.

"Mom—"

"Sssshhh. I need this book!" I said, giving Peyton the stink-eye to keep quiet. "And I'm going to see if I can buy it from him."

When the used car manager approached, he looked like he must have been duly forewarned. I held the book up. "How much do you want for this Billy Sunday book?"

Looking cautious like it was a trick question, he said, "It's not for sale."

"Not for sale!" Leaning forward in my seat I added, "Then where did you buy it? I *need* a copy."

"I found it in a used bookstore in Florida. It was the only one they had." The manager was still cautious, eyeing me like I might spring at him any moment.

"Well, I'm trying to find out about this man because he was a mentor to Billy Graham and I'm trying to discover why Graham was so fascinated by Billy Sunday and why he kept mentioning him in his autobiography. Why did *you* need this book?"

The young car salesman standing by looked like he had been shell-shocked as he took in "the crazy woman's" explanation, observing my exuberant passion while I tried to adroitly purchase the book from his boss. I'm sure he was also wondering if he was going to make a sale that day if the book couldn't be purchased. He more than likely saw dollar signs floating out the dealership doors — thinking he would very likely lose a commission.

After the used car manager saw I wasn't dangerous, only passionate, he quietly shared his story.

"I was on the road to nowhere. A drunk. And a drunk with no job. I felt led to go into this interesting looking used bookstore and there the Billy Sunday book sort of jumped out at me. I knew I was supposed to buy that book... that God had sent me in to buy it. So I did. And I read it.

"I discovered that Billy Sunday was a pro baseball player who liked to have a few drinks with the boys. He was a talented athlete but when he accepted Christ he quit baseball, quit drinking, and when he left the field, he began preaching the Gospel to anyone who would listen. He even preached to drunks lying in the gutter."

"And so now you use the book as a devotional in the mornings before you pray for a good workday, sending your car salesmen out to greet potential buyers?"

"Yes, ma'am."

"Well, I need that book. I'm willing to pay you for it."

I kept thinking there was much more in the book than he was telling me.

"And still, ma'am," the manager said, "my answer is the same. The book isn't for sale."

Knowing he meant what he said, I finally asked,

"Tell me, what made you leave Florida and come to Chattanooga after you read the book, accepted Christ, and dried out?"

He smiled then. "The Lord told me to come here. He said something big was going to be happening in the Tennessee Valley area."

"But He didn't tell you what?"

"No, He didn't."

After my family returned inside from car shopping, paperwork was completed on our purchases. The young salesman who'd helped us was floored because his very first sale ended up being a three-car deal. I suppose he guessed there really was something to praying before working and if he wasn't a dyed-in-the-wool believer before I walked in, perhaps he was after meeting the crazy woman trying to bargain for a book.

I drove home thinking, *What could it be —something big going to happen in the Tennessee Valley?* The only thing I could come up with was perhaps the ministries in the area were going to explode. Precept Ministries was located in Chattanooga and so was Ron Philips' Abba's House and ministry. Perry Stone's ministry was in Cleveland, Tennessee — thirty miles north — as was Judy Jacobs' ministry. Young Life meetings for teens were held at the McCallie Preparatory School.

Was there something more that I was missing?

I recalled that some of the Cherokee Native American

Indians — who used to live in and hunt up and down the Tennessee Valley before being sent on the Trail of Tears to Oklahoma around 1832 had returned to the Tennessee Valley area to meet up with those who had hidden in the mountains. In 1886, there was an outpouring of the Holy Spirit with a small group of Cherokees in this area. Later, the Pentecostal Church of God believers built their headquarters in the vicinity of Cleveland, Tennessee.

All of this had already happened. Was there truly something more?

I kept thinking about the Billy Sunday book. I thought I'd try one more time to check the internet for a copy and Eureka! I was finally in luck. A used bookstore in Florida had a copy of the book. *Florida again?* I quickly placed my order. When the book arrived, there was a note inside that read something like, "This book is not in top shape, so we're letting you have the book at a discount." Unwrapping the book, I found it to be in perfect shape considering it had been published in 1914. *And I received a discount?* Strange. I read the book but nothing of major import meant for me jumped out, though I found Sunday's story extremely powerful.

A couple of years later, I couldn't stop thinking about the used car manager and what God had told him about something big happening in my neck of the woods. Driving back to the dealership, I went in and asked to talk with the used car manager. He was no longer there it seemed. I asked, "Do you know where he went when he left?"

No one knew. In fact, when I described him, and his practice of praying with his salesman before work, no one recognized the man I described. And they all acted like they'd never heard of early-morning prayer meetings before work at their dealership. The young used car salesman was no longer there either. *So were those two men angels? Because no one had a clue who I was talking about!*

The entire episode is one of my unsolved mysteries and I'm still waiting to see what God does in the Tennessee Valley area.

CHAPTER 6

OUT OF OUR COMFORT ZONES

At one point, I seemed to be surrounded by people with cancer stories. I don't remember them all but I do recall two specific stories that made an impression.

Sarah walked into the salon with no pep. When she sat down for her appointment, she wasn't the friendliest of people, either. She was just — you know — kind of pushy and loud. She asked me to use personal tools she'd brought, which was totally fine with me. Continuing to speak in a harsh tone she let me know, "I have to use my own stuff because of this rare cancer in my leg."

As I was filing her nails I asked if she was in remission or in treatment. She said, "In remission for about a few years." I softly replied, "That's a blessing."

One word. There it was. That one little word changed her entire demeanor. Grabbing both of my hands, Sarah said, "Yes! Yes it is." And she began to tell me how she went to church as a kid but walked away from God in her twenties.

"I never thought I needed him" she said. "I had a great job, friends, money, a home...all that. Then a coworker invited me to a church event one day. I attended and soon found myself regularly attending. Around two years later I was diagnosed with a rare cancer in my leg. I got through it but I wouldn't have survived if God hadn't drawn me back to church. It was my refreshed faith that helped me fight the cancer to keep on believing."

A few days following Sarah's appointment, my husband — who is amazing by the way — sent a woman from his gym in my direction. Her name was Melanie and you guessed it: God had planned this appointment.

She walked in with the best hair and personality to boot. As I started her manicure I was recounting the several cancer stories I had recently heard. Sarah's story popped out of my mouth.

Melanie looked at me and said, "Wow. Why are you telling me this? My sister, Georgina, is fighting cancer and she's just like you. She's always talking about Jesus this and Jesus that and her faith in Him."

Melanie was perplexed about her sister's faith and battle with cancer. When I finally had the opportunity to meet Georgina one day, she was filled with light and she did love to chat about Jesus.

I love a Christmas story she shared with me. At the time of the story, her boyfriend had a serious drug addiction. He would usually take her money and leave to blow it all on drugs.

She told me, "Once, I hid money from my boyfriend

to buy the kids Christmas gifts. And one night, shortly before Christmas, I came home and discovered that he had found the money and taken it all.

"I traipsed out with the kids late that night to try and find him. While I drove around searching for him, the car broke down. And so did I. Crying out to God I said, 'Why is this happening? God! Please help me!'

"With a broken heart and now stranded, I sat there frantic about my plight. Soon, I noticed a pair of headlights behind me and saw a man approaching my car. As I rolled down the window, I discovered the man was none other than the one who sold me the car I was driving. He made a call and arranged for my car to be towed to the shop for a repair estimate. Not only did he pay for the repairs on my car, he gave me money to buy the kids' Christmas gifts."

It seems so ironic that we have miracles at Christmas, a time that represents when an event and miracle took place over 2,000 years ago. It didn't happen exactly on December 25th, but that is the day chosen to celebrate God coming down to hang out with His creation. To come in the most vulnerable state as a baby — a king in disguise no doubt — is such an unlikely way to present a Savior.

But as fantastical as it sounds, it was prophesied the Savior would come in just that form and fashion. *"All right then, the Lord himself will give you the sign. Look! The virgin will conceive a child! She will give birth to a son and will call him Immanuel (which means 'God is with us').*" Isaiah 7:14

Those who were waiting for that day and those who believed ancient scripture knew His worth and the prize we are still running to today. (John 1) They would have known that Immanuel means "God is with us."

Vicki also has a Christmas story to share.

It was bitter cold and below freezing outside. I was alone in my car in a Burger King parking lot waiting to dig into my bag for a nice hot-and-loaded cheeseburger with fries. I'd already spent Christmas with my family the weekend before and Christmas Eve would be spent writing and editing.

That's when I noticed that someone's car had died in the parking lot exit lane. Automobiles veered around the woman's car as her emergency lights flashed.

Upon further inspection, I saw her rear tire was flat. Surely some man who was strong enough to change a flat tire would pull over and help the woman who was now out of her car and checking her tire. Brrr!

With dark thirty full upon us, the lady again emerged from the vehicle, gimped back to her trunk to check for a spare, then slowly walked to the driver's side and eased back beneath the steering wheel, as if she was one hundred years old, although she looked younger.

Next, phone to her ear, she appeared to be calling for help. I knew of a service station nearby but couldn't recall the owner's name to check with information for a phone number. *Should I at least ask the woman if I could help in some way?*

Perhaps I could drive to the service station for help. After all, I was from the Volunteer State of Tennessee and had volunteered to help various people and organizations most of my life.

Sigh. *Not tonight Lord. Tonight, I simply do not want to volunteer. I want to eat in peace. Let someone else volunteer to help her.*

Making that declaration didn't stop memories from flooding in. I recalled how I'd felt after giving freely of my time. Better. But now, my stomach would feel much better if it was fed. Someone else could assist. Hot fries tempted. The cheeseburger assailed my senses and all but called my name.

That decision soon harbored guilt. The more I chewed, the more guilt piled on. *Wouldn't I want someone to help me if I was in her predicament?* Surely someone else would rise to the occasion. A big strong man who knew lots about jacks, lug nuts, and tire tools.

Over the next five minutes, drivers continued to whiz around the woman's car. "Why isn't someone stopping?" My question faded away into the dark.

While eating, I recalled having four flat tires myself.

The horror of those episodes was still fresh. During those times I'd been rescued by caring people. The last couple of times by men who changed out the tire; the scariest time by a woman and her son who stopped on the interstate, couldn't get the spare tire free, but then drove to a service station to send a tow truck back with help.

Internally struggling over this dilemma, I also recalled being accosted by a stranger the day before. Someone who'd followed me to my car parked in front of a strip mall and who'd aggressively asked for money. I'd thrown my gear stick in reverse, made my escape, and driven away thinking I might have been a possible robbery victim. I cringed to think the woman now stranded might try to set me up for a robbery. Helping others in these perilous times is scary. *But surely this woman couldn't have planned a flat tire in such a public place.* I popped another fry into my mouth, and wondered if I was reading too many newspapers and needed to curb thrillers. Then decided, no, I'd just been reading too many *local* newspapers.

Having finished my meal, I was now feeling this woman's pain. "Lord, tell me what to do. Should I volunteer to help or leave the job for someone else who may refuse to stop?" That's when I noticed the fast lube oil change franchise next door. Why hadn't I thought of them? Surely those guys working there knew how to do more than yell, "Bay one!" and change wiper blades.

Forming a plan, I drove directly behind the stranded vehicle and parked. Then locked my car to go and tap on the woman's window. "Hello? Ma'am? I'm wondering if you have someone coming to help you?" I heard another vehicle whiz past us while my teeth chattered from the wintry chill. *Why had I not worn a coat?* I made a mental note to start keeping a heavy coat in my car during the winter months.

The woman replied, "I've called my daughter and she's trying to find someone to help. I just bought this car and don't even know if it has a jack. Even if it has a jack, I can't change the tire because I recently had back surgery."

The panic in her voice died down to a pool of murky desperation. The temperature had dropped even more degrees below freezing and no way was I going to try to change her tire in the dark under such frigid conditions. Not only that, tire tools and I don't get along. I offered, "Next door is a business that provides oil changes. Perhaps they might change your tire if you check with them."

With a hanged-dog look the woman replied, "I don't have the money. I'll just have to wait to see if my daughter calls back."

Thinking of the last $20 bill in my purse and wondering if the woman was a con artist I said, "Well, just remember, you shouldn't run all of the gas out of your car trying to keep warm. You might need it to get home."

She thanked me profusely for stopping by to offer help. The banks were closed but while getting back into my car I kept thinking about that $20 in my purse. I could withdraw more cash the next day if I needed to — this woman, obviously, could not. I made the decision to drive over to the fast lube service station to see if they might possibly change out the tire. The hour was late. I looked at my watch. They were soon to close. Who knew what they charged to change a flat, but I had to ask and reasoned that asking didn't cost a dime.

Once inside, I pointed to the stranded car, explained the woman's dilemma —including her lack of money — to a young employee. At first he said, "We don't do tire changes. And we're closing." I countered with, "I have a twenty dollar bill. It's all I have with me. Will you consider changing her tire for $20?" The young man grinned. "I'll tell you what…ask the woman to limp her car over here and I'll put the car on the rack and change it out for her."

Thank you Jesus!

Victorious, I ran across the parking lot and knocked on the woman's window once more to share the good news, keeping the money arrangement to myself. She, too, was beside herself with joy and thanked me with ongoing enthusiasm.

Back to the fast lube service station to get my car, I was ready at last to part with my twenty. Surely I could get home without more mishaps and wouldn't need the cash. I said to the service attendant, "I really appreciate your helping this woman." Before I could dig into my purse to find my wallet, I saw the young man grin again.

"That's okay. I'm changing the tire for free."

Wanting to cry, kiss him, and hug him for being such a wonderful human being and great volunteer, I rethought my natural instincts and decided to offer my utmost thanks instead for his random act of kindness. This young man had worked all day and was ready for a break but instead he'd chosen to stay and help out. Heavenly angel in earth angel disguise?

Shivering from the cold, I hopped back into my car and drove away with a full tummy and a warmed heart knowing that if *I* stepped up and volunteered, my actions might encourage others to step up and volunteer as well.

My best takeaway from the experience was knowing that being from Tennessee —the Volunteer state — didn't have to be a prerequisite for volunteering. The prerequisite for volunteering was evident in the young man at the oil lube business. He was full of kindness with a willing heart. I was only the vessel God used to get the action of changing a tire for someone in motion. It was definitely a Merry Christmas for all. And God had once again *nailed it*. He'd arranged for key players to be in place to help this woman in her time of need.

CHAPTER 7

A RELENTLESS AND INDESCRIBABLE LOVE

One day I was told that Georgina, my beautiful friend with cancer, had been informed that her cancer had spread to her brain. Her situation had taken a turn for the worse. I remembered her coming in right after chemo with her hands full of fiery heat; it was hard to paint her nails but we managed to complete the process. And, we had another wonderful conversation.

She was awaiting an appointment at the end of the week to see if anything could be done about the hemorrhaging tumor now on her brain. I received a text from her sister, Melanie: "How can my sister still have so much faith and not be healed?"

I texted back: "You know, what's so great about following Jesus is that He changes our whole life perspective. When heaven becomes our reality and we know that we know it's our future eternal home, we can be at peace. When we truly understand this world's temporary state, heaven becomes more of a reality than being here."

A day or so later the Holy Spirit was really prompting me to go pray over Georgina. I texted her sis that morning but got no response. That is I got no response until I was going about my day and life, being busy and dropping kids off for all their activities.

The phone rang. It was Melanie. She said, "Nat, I wasn't going to have you over because Georgina is really sick. Then I felt that God was saying 'Why are you not letting people come over to pray?'"

I knew I had to drop what I was doing and immediately go pray for Georgina. This was serious business. So I called for backup. I phoned two amazing prayer warriors and we headed on over to Georgina's house. Truthfully, I had never actually prayed for someone to be healed before and I wasn't sure what to expect. But deep down, I knew God was in all of this. My prayer warrior team and I arrived and it felt like we prayed for only thirty minutes; but we actually prayed for over an hour. The time spent praying was beautiful and precious.

A few days later, I was home napping when my phone's notifications ping woke me. I'll never forget that text. "Nat, a miracle has happened! We went to the doctor today and he could not explain what he was seeing. The tumor that was bleeding in Georgina's brain is gone. Completely gone!"

I almost fell off my bed! I mean, I'd read about these miracles before and heard miraculous stories but never had I experienced such a thing through prayer. Even though the tumor had disappeared and the bleeding stopped, my beautiful sister only lived another seven to eight months. While Georgina was being taken care of by hospice I visited one day to take her some Bundt cakes. The hospice lady was such a Debbie Downer as Georgina introduced me as her sister. The woman was a bit confused as I am Hispanic and Georgina is African American. We laughed and said "sisters in Christ" and then I shared with the hospice worker about this journey Georgina and I'd had together.

The woman looked through her notes and seemed puzzled. She stammered out, "Wait. You had brain cancer too?"

"Yes," Georgina replied. "And nope, it never came back," we both piped out as the woman sat with disbelief shrouding her countenance. I found her reaction quite odd since she was a Christian hospice worker. Surely, she had seen God work miracles. Hmmmmm.

Then Georgina said, "I prayed that God would give me more time. Enough time for paperwork to go through so my sister, Melanie, could adopt my daughter."

My dear friend and sister in Christ passed away right after the adoption prayer was answered. God is relentless in His faithfulness, mercy and indescribable love.

You're probably thinking, "How can Natalie say that after Georgina passed away anyway?" *Easily.*

We all will die. Death is inevitable but while here we all have purpose. If we know Christ, we also know what's ahead. 1 Corinthians 2:9 tells us: *That is what the Scriptures mean when they say, "No eye has seen, nor ear has heard, and no mind has imagined what God has prepared for those who love him."*

Our hope, our future, and our goal — are to be at Home with our King.

Rest in beautiful peace my sweet sister Georgina, until I see you again.

CHAPTER 8

CONVICTION – KEEPING IT REAL

Let's lighten this up a bit with a funny story. One Sunday afternoon right after a rude client walked out of my nail bar, in walked a young woman. I was so annoyed by the previous person my attitude spilled over onto this poor woman, Judith. She had an appointment for a mani and pedi. As she sat down, my annoyance level raised even higher because of the thick gel polish she had on her nails that I had to remove.

In a rude tone, I said, "I'm going to have to charge you an extra fee for gel removal."

As we moved to the pedicure area my phone trilled. It was my daughter, so I informed Judith I would have to take the call and I excused myself.

When I returned she asked, "How old is your daughter?" I told her and discovered her daughter was the same age.

In my mind I had begun to tell myself, *Stop being a jerk. You don't even know this person.*

God also has quite the sense of humor. He is always making my ridiculous actions clear. It became evident this time when Judith then asked, "What did you and your girls do last night?"

My, oh, my! Now I wanted to sink into a hole because I thought, *Wow, you have been such a jerk and now you have to tell her you were at a mind-stopping Christian concert last night. How the wicked are brought to the light!*

The term for my predicament was called humbling.

So I told Judith about the concert and after that we had the best time as our conversation changed to a more upbeat discussion about faith. On her way out, she began to pay me and asked me how much the gel removal fee was. I bubbled over with nonstop laughter — like what she'd said was utterly ridiculous. I might have even rolled my eyes — and said, "Don't worry!" The minute I said that Jesus whispered, "Hmmmmmm. Really? Since when do you charge for gel removal?"

REALITY CHECK: *Never!*

I confessed to her about my day, and the mood the previous appointment had caused. And the appointment with her was redeemed. Nice!

Vicki has her own story about a reality check.

Working on this book with Natalie, I kept being bombarded by distractions. One day, my MS Word program acted devilish and I couldn't find my cursor for my Word document. It was at the bottom of my screen in the black space but wouldn't move up. I'd had that happen before, but couldn't recall how I fixed it. Spending time on my Ipad trying to figure it all out, I managed to get the mouse back. Then the document froze. I called my computer tech — a close friend — who told me how to shut it all down. Of course I would lose some information, but hopefully the damage wouldn't be too bad because autosave might come to my rescue. It did. I had to retype a few paragraphs, but that was all.

Then some other annoying things happened. I weathered all of this thinking, *The devil doesn't want this book out. He is in the details for sure. I'm going to ignore him and keep writing.*

But here was the real bugaboo. One day, writing like a mad woman, I stopped for lunch. I'd been trying to lose a few pounds and my daughter had ordered me some of the food from the diet plan she was on after having her last child. Her words when I last spoke with her were, "Mom, don't eat all the desserts the first week. You can have only a couple of snacks or desserts a day." Yeah. She knew me. I'd once tried that plan before and I ate all the desserts the first week. And were the chocolate bars with cherry ever so good!

Able to have lots of vegetables and four ounces of chicken, I decided to make a salad and throw in some olives and the chicken I'd cooked the day before. Then I planned on using salad vinegar with olive oil for a nice toss. After having broken the diet other days, this day I was being so good.

After taking a couple of bites of the lettuce, I savored the taste of the vinegar and oil dressing for a second but then for some reason, I looked down. There was something black in my salad. Pepper. No. I hadn't used pepper. Taking a closer look, the black thing was about the size of a quarter of my little finger. Too big for pepper kernels. Was that...wait...you bet. And the bug had antenna. Sticking my face almost in the bowl, there was something like a wisp of a tail coming out of the rear end of this odd looking bug.

Gross me out! I'd never seen a bug like that before. I didn't mind seeing a bug or two in the wild but I didn't want them in my house and I definitely didn't want them in my food! '

There went my salad. Right into the garbage. But then what about my chicken? Could I salvage the pieces?

Then it hit me. What all had that bug been doing in that salad before it died? Munching through the butter lettuce, everything going through its digestive system... and then I tossed everything with oil and vinegar! "Fantastic. God help me! Now I have no chicken! It will have to be thrown out too!"

Normally, during a full blown crisis and even smaller ones, I'm fairly calm. But this was disgusting and vile. Somebody should have to pay for this. And God wasn't helping that I could see. Justice! I wanted justice. After my week of annoying incidents and aggravation, this was the last straw.

Stomping to the kitchen, I dumped everything into the garbage and pulled the rest of the lettuce from the refrigerator. *I'm going to give somebody a piece of my mind. Who packaged this colossal hot mess?* At the same time, I'm hearing in my head, *Just calm down. Someone made a mistake. You've made mistakes before. You're a follower of Christ. Be nice.*

Humph!

I checked the package. At the bottom it read "Thoroughly Washed." *Those two words together! Are you kidding me!* Their humor was like pouring gasoline on a blue-hot flame.

Oh please!

What an insult! Now I was stewing. In full fury on the inside but no one would have known it from the outside, I started thinking up words like, disgusting. Vile. Nasty. Loathsome. Nauseating. Offensive. Queasy. Sickening. Ugh. And double Ugh! *Somebody is paying for all of this food I had to throw out and I'm giving them a piece of my mind to boot.*

Thank God the well known company had a high call volume that day handling other customers. I wondered if everyone else's Sweet Butter lettuce had dead bugs chilling around in the packaging. By the time a real person came on the line, my boil had eased off to a simmer and I remembered I was a Christian and my one goal was not to be a classic jerk. It wasn't the fault of the woman on the other end of the line in the complaint department. Poor woman. No way would I hold down her job.

So I stated the circumstances in the calmest voice I could muster. I think I recall saying something about the bug having antenna but she cut me off before I could get to the tail part and the body function of a bug's digestive system. "I am so sorry," she said, clearly understanding I was...er...disturbed. "Please give me the expiration date off the bag and where you bought the lettuce along with the number below the expiration date. Then give me your name and address and we'll send you some free coupons."

Free coupons — lady I expect an ocean cruise with plenty of cherry chocolate cake!

Without making myself sound too crazy I replied, "Please make sure you also throw in enough coupons to cover the cost of the chicken I had to throw out too."

Without hesitation she added, "We sure will!"

If I hadn't had enough time to cool down before the woman came on the line, I might have embarrassed myself by asking for a free week in the best digs in Santorini and a year's worth of coupon therapy with a local psychiatrist.

So now, there was salve on my feelings but no food in my belly. My writing time had been thwarted.

You can guess what happened next.

Bring on the brownies!

At least I'd managed to curb my tongue and not take out my disgust and frustration on someone else. Though I must say, it will be quite some time before I can eat lettuce again. And you can bet my "thoroughly washed" Sweet Butter lettuce will get a second bath before I throw in a chicken!

And why was I reacting like this over a bug, I wondered. Normally, I'd have thrown the food out and gone about my business without calling the company because I could only imagine the thousands upon thousands who call companies like this to get free coupons when they haven't truly been traumatized by an insect in their food.

Perhaps it was overload from my aggravating week plus the computer problems. Perhaps the devil was in the details since he loves to mess with humans to distract us. Or perhaps God was allowing me to be tested so I'd be reminded of this verse:

Sensible people control their temper; they earn respect by overlooking wrongs. Proverbs 19:11

All I know for sure is that aggravations and setbacks are for a moment. How I deal with those moments in time show others how I try to live as a Christian. Not only will others know us by the fruit we produce, they'll know us by our behavior. Sometimes I fail at being a "good Christian," especially when provoked. But being a Christ follower means if I repent and move forward and keep learning from experiences that are either bad or unfortunate, I get a second chance. God is all about those second chances.

And later when I thought about my ordeal with the Sweet Butter lettuce and the bug and my thinking, "Somebody is paying for this," I couldn't help but think that *somebody* had to pay for my mess-ups as well, whether accidental or intentional.

His name is Jesus. Without His being nailed to the cross and His shedding of blood, my sins could have never been forgiven. There had to be atonement and God's way for the atoning of sin in the Last Days was through the perfect and ultimate sacrifice of His One and Only Son. The perfect Lamb of God.

CHAPTER 9

FREEDOM FROM HOLDING ON

Do you have time for some more stories?

I always thought about writing this book and I wondered if anyone would want to read about my little life. I honestly don't know how my experiences will be viewed, however, I do know this: Many wander around wondering about this Christian life thing. I often hear, "Well, this person says they're Christian but did this, or this church did that, this pastor cheated, and on and on. I hope while I have your attention you take one thing to heart: God did not make any of this mess down here. Mankind did.

I believe the biggest struggle we face has to do with God's sovereignty and our free will. The buildings that many of us call "church" are just that — buildings. What's inside the Church, the people — the drug addicts now set free, the prostitute now redeemed, the thief now made new, the orphan who now has a father, the outcast who is now seen and the list goes on — are the Church. Christians. And Christians are broken and will always be broken pieces being put back together.

Jesus said in John 3:17, *"God sent his Son into the world not to judge the world, but to save the world through him."*

If I could say one thing to the world — if I had perhaps two minutes to address the world as a whole, I would say, "Don't put Christians on a pedestal for we will forever fail you. But sweet Jesus never will."

How do I know? To learn the answer to that question, read on.

Is it possible that God would align all the nail appointments I had one day? Could He have really put my schedule together so perfectly that day...like a sun rises and sets? I believe so. When I think back, the circumstances were unbelievable and I could never have prepared the outcome. For instance, I worked on Sundays only on rare occasions. This was one of them.

As Stacy sat down for her pedicure she apologized for missing her appointment several months earlier. I laughed. "Due to all the coupon clients I didn't even remember you missed it!"

Still, she wanted to tell me why she missed her appointment that day. "I'm a hardcore mom. I always make my son come straight home after school to focus on homework. I never let him hang around with friends really, because I always worried about him getting straight A's in preparation for college. He had a half-day one day, and asked to ride his bike with friends to

Starbucks. He called and asked to go a little further down the road to Target. I agreed and asked him to head home right afterwards. He called to let me know he was on his way home. Minutes later, I received a call from my boyfriend telling me my son was being airlifted to Children's Hospital. I was in disbelief. I'd just spoken to my child.

"He was struck by a truck running a red light."

What she said next gives me chills even as I write her story: "But you know what? God was in this situation the whole time. The second driver was an off-duty paramedic who immediately started working on my son. But the third driver in the accident was a mom who had lost her daughter in the same way. This woman ran to my son's side and prayed. In fact, she prayed with my child the entire way to the hospital.

"When I arrived at Children's Hospital, a huge group from my church was already there praying. A pediatric neurosurgeon was at Children's from Los Angeles to drop off paperwork. He'd heard the call come in and prepared to work on my son. The diagnosis: no eyesight, and most likely, severe brain damage. But after some time and many months of prayer my son woke up from his coma and walked out of the hospital with all injuries healed."

My favorite part of her story was this: She said, "God spoke to me through this event and reminded me not to hold onto something so tightly — something that was only temporarily mine."

It's a powerful message, isn't it? We humans want so much to hold on to people and things — but those people and things aren't truly ours to begin with. That's where Jesus comes in. He offers us freedom from all of the "holding on."

John 8:36 (KJV) tells us He said, *"If the Son therefore shall make you free, ye shall be free indeed."*

My next appointments were a woman from India and her neighbor from Russia. As I began the first pedicure they were chatting about life and their kids. The woman from India asked me if I had any children.

"Yes. I have three teenage daughters.

She gasped. "How are you even alive? I have *one* and I am going *crazy*."

It was not because of what you might think, either. The woman was actually making herself crazy because she worried so much about controlling her daughter's life. She even mentioned not being able to sit and enjoy dinner with her husband because she was worried her daughter wasn't doing homework upstairs. She mentioned college, which was funny, but actually not. She said, "Oh no! If she goes away to college I will follow her and make sure she is doing what she needs to be doing."

The scenario was stifling.

I shared my freedom with her regarding my daughters. "I am at ease for two reasons: First, our kids are only kids once. After that they are adults. I want them to enjoy being kids without all the pressure. Second, I believe in God and that He has a plan for them so my hope is they will learn to trust Him and have faith.

Her friend agreed with me, and the moment was sweet.

I then told her that I thought God had brought a previous client in just for her. I told her the woman's story about her son and her faith. My client didn't have much to say at the end of the story but on her way out I said, "Maybe today, you can just go home and enjoy your daughter. Hang out and give her a hug."

A firm believer in Godcidents, I do believe with all my heart that God arranged those two appointments almost back to back because He wanted to use me to reveal His love to others.

On another note, I don't want to scare anyone with the whole topic of hell but I'd be a hypocrite if I wholly believe in the Bible and leave that part out. Stick with me for a minute.

This next appointment was the nicest lady from Canada. I'll call her Judy. Judy was telling me about her son and how bad his asthma was. After she finished I mentioned how the day before, at my friend's church, a woman shared a story about her son and his asthma. Judy smiled and shared that she wasn't sure about faith, God, and all the rest. I don't recall every word of the conversation but I do clearly recall the rest of the day. As I was heading out, my husband texted me about my eldest daughter's birth certificate. He needed it for softball but he couldn't locate it. As I drove home to look, I wholeheartedly asked the lord, "God, that lady was just so nice. Do you really say if she doesn't believe in Jesus she will go to hell?"

Yep. I was that blunt. I put it out there because my heart hurt at the thought. She was so sweet while visiting with me, and if she wasn't saved in Christ, I'd never see her again.

Arriving home, I went to my closet to look for the birth certificate in a basket I kept there. I could not find it so I lifted the basket up. I couldn't believe my eyes. There it was loud and clear, the answer to my question — an envelope with a CD inside that had been placed on my car window years earlier. I couldn't move because in Sharpie written on the envelope it read "HEAVEN and HELL are REAL!" *Are you kidding me? I'd just asked God about this!*

Honestly, I was stunned. I ran to my daughter's room to listen to the CD I'd thrown beneath the basket long ago…and found the day my heart was so troubled.

The CD was actually an audio book about a woman who had traveled to America from a different country. She began attending church and kept praying, asking God if heaven and hell were real. She claimed God gave her a vision of both places.

That's all I listened to, just enough to hear and think that God of the whole universe had answered me once again, nailing my request to suit my need at that particular time, giving me answers to my questions.

I believe there are no coincidences, only Godcidents.

Now read a chilling story of Vicki's.

Ever since I was a small child and learned about Christ and heaven and hell, I never doubted heaven and hell being real places. For me, I couldn't have one without the other. If I was going to believe such an incredible story that Christ died for me so I could have eternal life, I couldn't cherry pick parts of the story for truth and not accept the whole story in its entirety. If Jesus said, "*I am the way, the truth, and the life. No one can come to the Father except through me*" (John 14:6), I had to believe those other words Jesus claimed to be true. For example: *God saved you by his grace when you believed. And you can't take credit for this; it is a gift from God. Salvation is not a reward for the good things we have done, so none of us can boast about it.* (Ephesians 2:8-9)

If Jesus and His disciples taught that works and simply being a good person doing good works won't get a soul into heaven, I had to believe that too. John 10:9 tells us Jesus said, "*Yes, I am the gate. Those who come in through me will be saved. They will come and go freely and will find good pastures."*

As an adult, I discovered many things that convinced me even more that the hell part was as real as the heaven part. The puzzle pieces of the Bible all fit together. The Bible is like a novel. It starts with a hook, has a riveting middle, and a dynamite ending. And after studying the Bible inductively, I decided there's no way that many people could write that many chapters over a period of that many years, and have a satisfactory ending. There's a continuous thread throughout the Bible and there are prophecies that were written that didn't come true until hundreds of years later. So I believed the Bible first on faith, and then on research and study.

Plus, rocks don't lie. Discoveries are still being made in Israel that prove the Bible true.

But, back to my childhood.

In my late teens, I discovered my mother's future cardiologist, Dr. Maurice Rawlings, had written a book, *Beyond Death's Door*. I read it cover to cover. More than that. Let's just say I inhaled his book in one sitting, then dog-eared some pages.

Dr. Rawlings admitted he'd been a sit-on-the-pew-bench kind of Christian, lukewarm in his religion... until he kept dealing with patients who, after being shocked back to life, told one of two stories: While they were out cold going through an NDE (near death experience), they'd been in either heaven or hell. After being shocked back to life, many told Dr. Rawlings about their experiences. One man was shocked back to life several times. Dr. Rawlings wrote, "Each time he regained heartbeat and respiration, the patient screamed, 'I am in hell!' He was terrified and pleaded with me to help him. I was scared to death. In fact, this episode literally scared the hell out of me!"

Finally, Dr. Rawlings said a simple prayer over the man and asked to be left alone to do his work, and the last jolt of the electrified paddles kept the patient alive. Later, when the patient was able to tell his tale, not only was it riveting, it was terrifying enough to prompt Dr. Rawlings — a cardiologist at the cutting edge of resuscitation — to write his book about death and what could possibly be in store depending on whether one is a believer or not. The book then became a televised documentary and to this day can be viewed on YouTube.

Many years later, a couple of books were published by people who said they had died and spent time in heaven before coming back to life to tell their story. One story, *90 Minutes in Heaven* by Don Piper and Cecil Murphey, was made into a movie. Another book produced as a film was *Heaven Is for Real* by Todd Burpo. I read both and any other books about NDEs I could get my hands on.

During my avid research on the subject of heaven and hell, I was fortunate to meet a man who claimed he'd also died and gone to heaven for four hours. Lonnie

Honeycutt claimed he died with Stage IV cancer, spent time in heaven, and was healed and allowed to come back to earth. Fantastical, I know. But his story, along with photos of his tortured and cancerous body, were convincing.

When Cecil Murphey was compiling stories for a book he and Twila Belk were publishing titled *I Believe in Heaven,* I received permission from Lonnie to condense his story to 750 words for their book. What convinced me that Lonnie's story was indeed true was his reaction when telling his story in person. He became visibly upset when describing hell — a place he was allowed to see from heaven — for a persistent woman who kept asking him questions about it. At one point, tears formed and he could hardly continue. With Lonnie's permission, I've included a short form of his story previously published in *I Believe in Heaven.*

THE HINGE POINT
by
Lonnie Honeycutt
with Vicki H. Moss

Many patients die during surgery, rush through a dark tunnel, see a brilliant light, then find themselves at the pearly gates. I suffered from Stage IV cancer — one of the worst stages and grades possible — was pronounced brain dead, and found myself in the company of angels.

But first, let's back up. In 2003 I visited my doctor complaining of a swollen lymph node. Prescribed a round of steroids and antibiotics, I was instructed to "watch it." Within months, I was back in the doctor's office and diagnosed with cancer.

Some of my tumors were larger than a golf ball, though more elongated. Aggressive treatment began on November 14, 2007, and 40 radiation treatments plus concurrent chemotherapies were penciled on my calendar. I developed a rash that ran from the top of my head to my feet. Pustules covered my body; the skin on my head became so brittle that when I vomited, blood poured through broken skin of my scalp. I lost my beard. Photoaging (dermatoheliosis) caused my skin to lose integrity and wrinkled my face and neck. Voice gone from loss of saliva, I was also left with no taste buds.

One night, I fell asleep in my son's bed. When my wife checked on me the next morning, my body was blue with only a faint pulse. When paramedics arrived, my wife asked, "Is he going to make it?" The paramedic replied, "It doesn't look good for him."

At the hospital, friends gathered outside to pray while my wife was told, "Your husband's brain is hypoxic-anoxic. There is no flow of oxygen to his brain. He's brain dead."

I died. It was February 16, 2008.

My memories of heaven began with being immediately transported to a road of transparent gold where I was flanked by three angels — one on either side and one behind me. I guesstimated the angels were between six-and-a-half and seven-feet tall. All four of us wore traditional flowing white robes; garments a first century person might have worn. One angel was black like onyx or ebony — not merely black but the blackest of black. The other two were more olive complexioned, yet, complexions had nothing to do with their inner natures. And, the angels who accompanied me were of no particular ethnicity.

Along with clean and fresh air, the sky was an amazing array of blue and white. I initially assumed the white was due to clouds, however, closer observation proved I was watching a myriad of angels. As my escorts and I walked, countless angel legions flew to and fro. Their ranks stretched as far as my eyes could see in all directions and I realized my vision was much better than it had been on Earth. I longed to reach the city I could see in the distance.

A massive number of people had gathered awaiting my arrival at the entrance of the city. Upon closer inspection, I saw people gathering at arched windows similar to those in Spanish-style homes. Spires, bridges, walkways, and gardens with beautiful flowers and trees were located where people strolled along pathways.

I was not only aware of people on Earth, I was also aware of those in hell.

I've been asked: "How could you see Earth from Heaven?" And, I must admit, words fail to allow me to describe exactly how I saw events taking place. If I had to try to describe the manner in which I was viewing the happenings on Earth and in hell, it was like looking through a thin, extremely pale membrane or veil. I knew what people were doing, could see my wife and people on Earth praying for me, and I could also hear those who prayed for me.

As I walked with my escort of angels, I turned to look behind them and then downward toward our feet. There were no shadows — none under us, none behind us or in front of us, none around the trees or the flowers that lined the sides of the road. Shadows simply didn't exist in Heaven.

While on this road, I also experienced something I've rarely experienced here on Earth and that is…peace. Peace that is literally far beyond human comprehension. I saw people I knew — those on Earth who'd helped guide me along my spiritual journey.

One woman I somehow instantly recognized wore a blue dress with puffy sleeves and had a personal message for Dawn.

The most unforgettable and remarkable thing I remember from my trip to Heaven was the *feeling* I felt from the people who waited for me to cross the threshold into the city. To describe the *feeling* best — I felt a pressure, but I knew exactly what it was the people were feeling. Giddy! Absolutely excited about the fact I was coming to join them and that I would be spending the rest of eternity with them and Christ. The feeling was palpable. The pressure — tangible.

I do not remember meeting Jesus. I do know this: I was asked by someone — possibly the Holy Spirit or Jesus Himself — if I wanted to stay or return to Earth. I thought of Dawn, my grieving wife in the hospital room, and said, "Yes, I want to return to Earth."

After I returned to Earth, I described the woman I met in heaven to Dawn. I repeated the message she'd given me. Only Dawn would have understood the message; it was from her mother, June. My wife knew I had truly been to heaven because I hadn't known her mother as a 35-ish year-old woman. I'd only known her in her twilight years. She found a faded photo— one I don't recall ever having seen before — and she showed it to me. It was the same woman.

Thea, Dawn's cousin, heard about my meeting June. After hearing the details of the blue dress with puffy sleeves, Thea said, "That was Aunt June. I know that dress. Aunt June was thin, and I told her that because of the puffy sleeves, the blue dress looked too big on her."

Since my return, I know my experience was as real as anything I've ever experienced before in my life…and the amazing time spent in an awesome heaven never fades.

What I also know for certain: God is moved by prayers of the saints — anyone who has accepted Jesus as personal Savior.

Note: Pastor Lonnie Honeycutt lives in Mobile, Alabama, pastors 99 for 1 Ministries, is a Stage IV cancer survivor and has authored two books: *Death, Heaven and Back* and *Living Jesus Out Loud*. See www.99for1Ministries.com or www.LivingJesusOutLoud.com.

CHAPTER 10

YOU ARE NOT ALONE

Teeni's story is one of my favorites. She walked in one evening with the online coupon and a little bit of attitude. Not rudeness, just a bit of a hard shell, and I thought *boy oh boy, there I am a few years back.*

She began to come in every two weeks, and each time the Holy Spirit equipped me by bringing stories to mind to share with her.

On one of those nights, Teeni told me, "You know, I really don't know if I believe."

Chuckling, I said, "You don't believe my stories? I promise, I am not creative enough to make these up." She laughed too, so with hesitancy, I added, "Oh. You don't know if you believe in *God?*"

"Yeah," she said. Then I told her about my hummingbirds — a story I'll share later. When I was done, she looked at me and said, "This is crazy. My grandma sits by this window and these hummingbirds zoom in and she begins crying. It happens all the time."

"Well, go ask your grandma and I bet she will say the hummingbirds are from Jesus." When she came back, she told me that she'd asked her grandma and yes, the hummingbird visitations were linked with God.

Then, I didn't see Teeni for quite a while. During this time period I began working at a different salon. I sold another coupon ad while working there, and Teeni managed to get one and returned for my services. Once again, Jesus was the topic of many conversations.

One day, Teeni asked me the difference between a Christian and a Catholic. I simply replied, "Christians focus on a personal relationship with Jesus, a lifestyle to be Christ-like in every way, however, that doesn't mean all Christians I know are like that. For me though, it's just that simple.

"Jesus revealed my deepest dark places and showered forgiveness into them. He made me literally fall in love with Him with a relationship that is as real as your and my breathing. I can even feel His presence. It's a feeling that is so wonderful my heart races and tears fall at the very thought of Him. Just like any other relationship I have with a person I can see, this relationship with Jesus is one that is real and I can *feel* it as well."

One day, Teeni messaged me and asked if I would come in that Sunday for her. I usually didn't work Sundays, but I came up with a plan, so I said yes. At the end of the appointment, I said, "Hey, it's Sunday. And I'm headed to church. It's down the street. Want to come?" She said, "Oh no — I have plans already. Maybe another time."

"Okay," I replied. "But the door's always open for you to come with me." And we parted.

A few weeks later Teeni came in laughing. "Guess what? Last time when you invited me to go to church with you, as I drove out of the parking lot, my friend messaged me to cancel our plans. I paused, and thought, *God are you telling me to go to church with Natalie?*"

"Well, why didn't you come?" I asked.

She laughed again. "I know. But instead of going to church with you, I made my friend keep our plans."

Later, once again Teeni messaged me for a Sunday appointment. Again, I said yes…and smiled to myself as I hatched another plan.

This time Teeni was all dressed up when she arrived and I commented on it.

"Yeah. I had a bad day and night so I decided to dress up to make myself feel better."

At the end of this appointment, I again invited her to church. And this time *drum roll* she came. She began attending every Sunday and soon brought her best friend. Simply wonderful!

I even arranged a date for her with my cousin because she was so beautiful and fun and seeking Jesus, and was a good match for my cousin because he, too, knew Jesus.

Teeni and I began to pray during some appointments. I showed her how to download a Bible app and how to find what to read. God was truly moving in her life.

Then a time came when I left that salon and even stopped doing nails for a bit. But that didn't deter my outreach. I started inviting Teeni and her best friend over to my house for "nails and chatting" and gave them the little devotional and a book titled *When God Winks*.

Soon, I moved to a different church, our paths went a different way, and Teeni and her friend were out of my life about a year or so. Then in 2015 I received a text from Teeni. She told me her grandma was being taken care of by hospice and her whole family was with her grandma praying. She said, "All the prayers are in Spanish and I'm not sure what they are saying. Can you come over and pray with me?"

Without hesitating, I drove over that very day. The time spent was wonderful. Teeni and I sat on her grandma's porch and she had many questions for me about Jesus. Hummingbirds were even flying around the entire time. Then her aunt asked me to come in with the family and pray. Yep. Just like God to pull me out of my comfort zone. I did go in to pray with them. And later in the day, I had the privilege of sitting with Teeni some more on that porch to encourage her and let her know that even when God's children walk away from God, He never walks away from them. I drove away overwhelmed from my emotions thinking, *Who am I — just a manicurist — that Teeni would even think of calling me during her time of need, because of Jesus.*

What an amazing privilege and humbling experience on a beautiful day to be sitting on Teeni's grandma's porch as she was soon to be with her Lord. I'll never forget that special time of being allowed to share about Jesus, especially after I texted her with encouragement from the Bible a few days after her grandma's passing.

What happened next, on the morning of December 27th, was quite the shock, though. I received a text from Teeni's best friend informing me that the beautiful, super woman I'd come to know was gone. She'd passed away in her sleep.

Every time I write about Teeni, salty hot tears flow and I'm in awe of God because He knew Teeni's time span and He'd placed us together for some beautiful fun and amazing times. Teeni had become a forever friend and even though our friendship was cut short, He knew I would see her again. God's handprints had been all over our relationship.

Of course, I don't know why she had to go so soon, but I do know that because I have an eternal perspective over this temporary life, I am hopeful and joyful I will get to see her again.

And the hummingbirds in this story? Of course you want to know how they figure in.

So one day I was sitting at my station in the salon — which faced the window — and I saw a hummingbird. *Hmmmm, I've never really seen or noticed a hummingbird here before.* The next day I was on break outside by my car talking on my cell phone when I noticed another hummingbird. Then another. And another. And later that night, I was in the shopping center parking lot on the phone again when one flew in front of my windshield.

I told my friend Meg — yes, the Meg from an earlier story— "Hey, lately when I've been chatting about Jesus, I keep seeing hummingbirds." She gasped. Then said, "What? You're so freaky!" And she laughed.

I replied, "What do you mean?"

Meg said, "Hummingbirds are often around me in my backyard when I am praying."

I remembered my aunt had an amazing hummingbird story but I couldn't recall all of the details so I ended my phone call with Meg and called my aunt. Soon after the chat with my aunt, I began noticing two hummingbirds who had taken up residence in a tree in my backyard. I'd lived there four years and had never before seen them. My senses began tuning into the delicate hummingbirds and their sounds. I noticed that one individual sang especially loud and I soon began sitting outside for long periods of time, noticing the habits of these fine feathered friends. I chuckled and thought, *Well, if Jesus is hanging around in these little birds, surely I should feed Him.* So I bought a feeder and loved sitting in the backyard watching those tiny creatures.

Then the storm came. Life often brings different kinds of storms. One day, I'd begun to fill with sadness. When I arrived home from work, a sermon popped up on my Facebook wall. I clicked "play." As I listened, I stood in the rain in my backyard, amazed throughout the whole sermon. I was not alone. I was with a friend. My little loud hummingbird. That tiny creature didn't move the entire time the sermon played. So amazing. Like she was listening with me.

A few days later, again saddened and brokenhearted about my husband's job loss and having to move again, I sat in my backyard looking for my little bird friends. While I looked for them, a worship song began playing: "You Are Not Alone."

As I listened to the words I heard the singing of that little bird as if it were singing the same tune. I know this sounds farfetched, but truly, it flew out from the tree and I heard the Lord whisper to my heart, *I sent these as a sign that I am always with you.* To this day I see them everywhere I go — literally everywhere — all the time.

I'm not the only one with a hummingbird story. Vicki has one to share as well.

Natalie's hummingbird story reminded me of my own hummingbird tale. My parents had an incredible view off of their mountaintop back porch in Alabama. It was there they rested after a long day's work and took in the view of the valley below. As they rocked in sturdy rocking chairs, they recalled stories from their childhood.

Growing up together in the cove below the mountain, they had plenty of stories to share. While chatting about one thing or another, they noticed beautiful ruby throated hummingbirds flying in to drink the nectar from Rose of Sharon blossoms — blossoms on trees mother had planted near the porch. One day, they decided to buy a couple of hummingbird feeders to hang from the porch roof so they could more closely observe the darling critters. Daddy seemed to enjoy them most of all and kept the feeders filled with sugar water. He sat out on the porch for hours watching riotous sunsets and listening to the whirring noises hummingbirds make while hovering and feeding with wings beating furiously.

But eventually the day came when Mother was no longer with him. She'd taken her leave of this aging world and had gone to be with her Lord and King. She'd been a poor wayfaring stranger on this planet and her time to leave had come.

On that day, Daddy lost interest in riotous sunsets and the beating wings of darting hummingbirds. He no longer sat on the porch or filled the hummingbird feeders.

I once asked, "Daddy, would you like for me to fill the hummingbird feeders for you?" His reply had been a sad and forlorn, "No thanks." Though we never discussed it further, I wondered if perhaps the ruby throated hummingbirds reminded him too much of his wife whose name was Ruby Evelyn. Daddy had become so saddened and lost from Mother's leaving him that he could hardly function. During one day of reminiscing he told me, "I wish I'd passed before your Mother."

After Daddy died several years later and went to be with Jesus and the love of his life, I often thought about him and wondered if he was now happy again. I frequently dreamed about him. In one dream, I asked, "Daddy, is heaven as you thought it would be?" He replied, "Yes."

During this time of frequently dreaming about my parents, mostly Daddy, I was in my bedroom sitting on my bed, typing on my computer, trying to meet a writing deadline. Before me, several feet away, was a set of French doors. Within my line of vision, I suddenly saw something dart around outside the doors' glass.

Looking up to see what was making such a commotion, I saw a ruby throated hummingbird staring back at me, watching my every move. The creature flew to the middle of the glass in one door, and suspended himself as his wings furiously beat the air to keep him aloft. Bold. This tiny thing was bold. And staring me down! *What do you want?* Stunned, my first thoughts were, *I have never seen a hummingbird on this farm and I've lived here for over eighteen years. Where did this tiny bird come from? Why are you here staring at me little bird?*

What popped into my conscience at that time was that this little bird was telling me to rest assured, Daddy was fine. Amazing! And I felt an overwhelming sensation that this feathered friend's visitation was from the Lord. I no longer had to worry if Daddy was happy or not. And nine years later, strangely enough, I have yet to see another hummingbird on my property.

I know that Numbers 22:28 tells us God opened the mouth of a donkey to speak. So why couldn't He send hummingbirds for reassurance? He created them. God can do anything.

CHAPTER 11

DREAM BIG

After a year of amazement and growth, I heard the Lord say to me that my time at that salon was finished. I kept hearing Him tell me this, yet I was afraid to call it quits there. One sure way I knew He wanted to move me was He completely dried up the well, forcing me to go in another direction. In other words, my income dwindled until I was unable to pay rent for that station.

I soon discovered an empty room in the same building where my mom worked as an esthetician. The rent for the room was $100 less than what I had been paying and was a naked canvas. I thought, *How perfect! I can finally decorate a place according to my tastes and meet with people in privacy one on one.* So I walked through the open door in front of me praying and trusting the whole way. I even sold my expensive handbag to pay for the paint and decor.

After giving notice, I headed out the door and into my dream place. Staying after work hours, I cleaned and painted until about 1 A.M. Within a few days, my new work abode was ready. Still in need of a chair and a sink, I also needed a few miracles. The chair I had set my sights on cost $50. But where would the money come from?

In walked Kimberly, a regular. I never raised my prices on this awesome client/sister in Christ or charged her extra for nail art because with such a friend, it's never really about the money. So per usual, she handed me a $25 check at the end of her appointment. After stopping at the restroom on her way, she returned to my room and placed a $50 bill on my table. I couldn't believe it. "Whoah! What's this for?"

"I was in the restroom," Kimberly said, "and Jesus said to give you this $50 because you needed it." Of course, I was grinning big.

I'm not the only one who's had an experience like the one with Kimberly. Vicki has, too.

Rose, a woman at a church I was visiting was smack dab in the middle of a messy divorce. The pastor prayed for Rose and asked the rest of us to keep her in our prayers. Later, at home, I heard the Lord telling me to give her $100. I laughed. Out loud. And said, "Lord, right now I don't have $100, but if you give me $100 to give to Rose, I will."

Immediately, the Lord told me to go to my desk in the kitchen. I didn't hear an audible voice, but the message was one I suddenly heard in my spirit. So I went. There was some paperwork there that needed sorting out —

folders and manila envelopes I hadn't looked through in years. As I was cleaning out and deciding what needed to be kept and what needed to be thrown away, I found a white envelope. Inside was a note and $140 cash, in ten dollar bills. The note reminded me that this was the cash collected from the parents of the children in my daughter's elementary grade class when I was a homeroom mother. I'd written a check to the teacher for the money collected, and had never deposited the cash in my checking account. This was *my* money. And the money had rested in an envelope for eight years until God had a specific use for it.

But there it was. One hundred dollars for the woman going through hard times and $40 left over for me. I was so stunned by this episode of God's provision that I ended up spending the $40 on food for Rose and her child as well, by way of a breakfast and shared dinner. We had a lovely time getting to know one another during the dinner at her home.

But the story gets better. The Lord also told the recipient of my money — which is all really the Lord's money since He's my true provider — to give another lady who was going through devastating times a bouquet of flowers to cheer her. "I didn't have the money to buy the flowers until you gifted me with the $100," Rose said. "Unbelievable how God provides and uses us to help others!"

I agreed.

Yes, some of these stories are unbelievable. But to those of us God has spoken to with specific directions and orders, these happenings or *Godcidents* are very believable. And most of us are still in awe. In awe because of His magnificence, yes, but we should not be surprised that these events are taking place in this day and age. Jesus told us what to expect after He left Earth to be with His Father, *"I tell you the truth, anyone who believes in me will do the same works I have done, and even greater works, because I am going to be with the Father."* (John 14:12)

So here's some food for thought: Why aren't we Christians asking for more Godcidents? Big ones. We all should be dreaming big and asking big to glorify His name!

CHAPTER 12

LIGHT ENTERS IN

The morning after the day of the incredible tip, I received a phone call from the owner of the space I had rented. He told me the woman down the hall said she had an allergy to nail products. I replied that I didn't do artificial nails and there would be no way she could smell anything.

The following day I was alone in my rented space and the only thing odiferous was a lit candle as I had no clients yet. The owner of my rental space called me asking if I was at the salon. "Yes, I'm here," I replied.

"The lady I told you about who complained about her allergies called. She's complaining of an odor," he said.

"Impossible," I replied. "I've yet to receive clients."

The next morning I got another call. He said I would have to move to the downstairs portion of the salon. I declined. "I gave up my other station and moving my clients isn't fair since you knew from the get-go that I'd be doing nails. But let me get back with you."

As I drove away, I pulled my car over and came to a stop, yelling at God. Yes, I did. "God! What are you doing? You made this new venture so clear and you have provided. I don't understand!"

The next day I declined moving to another location. My reply was that I would gather up my things and leave. That afternoon I called Christa, my dear friend, and ran my dilemma by her. This was her response: "There are three scenarios. First is that God didn't tell you to move, you just thought He did." In my mind I was thinking, *No way! God's instructions were so clear.*

But then Christa continued. "Second, Natalie, the enemy saw your light enter and didn't like it."

I thought, *Yeah, that woman dreaming up smells is clearly the enemy.*

"Third," Christa said, now on a roll (and as soon as she gave me the third point my heart was overwhelmed because I knew God was in the mix and had nailed it) "God said, 'Here it is. The salon you've been dreaming of. Now, if I take it all away, will you still follow me with all your heart?"

Hmmmmmmmmmm so crazy! So hard and so amazing all at once. You know Jesus, I'm ALL IN!

My schedule was empty the next week until Friday. So I said a prayer in pure faith. "Okay Lord, I'm not looking for my next salon, I'm going to wait for you to show me where to go. I am going to trust that you will place me in a salon by Friday! So I waited and didn't call one single client — trusting He would open a door. And to my sheer delight, He did.

Tuesday, I drove to the store to grab a bottled water

and snack to eat during my daughter's softball game. I had to use the restroom but the one at the store was broken. This is funny but I gotta share this part so hang with me. I got in my car with my youngest daughter and we drove by a soccer field. I pulled over because I knew the restroom there was nicer than the one at school. As I made my left turn, I noticed a small green truck sitting at the stop sign. When turning in front of the truck, I spotted the driver waving his hand and pointing at the hood of my car. I pulled into the parking lot of the convenience store and got out to look at the hood but saw nothing wrong. The truck pulled in next to me and I counted three young guys inside. The driver said, "Hi! We're all brothers. Christians. And I'd like to do something nice for you. I'd like to fix the dent in the hood of your car for free."

I could hardly believe his offer and said, "I don't care about this dent, however, you can do something. Pray for me and my work." The brother sitting in the middle said, "Okay." All three took off their hats, held hands, and the young man prayed for me like he knew me and knew exactly what I needed in the way of prayer. The moment was surreal and when the brothers finished praying, I asked, "Do you do this all day? Just drive around asking people if you can pray for them?"

One brother replied, "We are simply filthy rags and nothing more than servants of Jesus." Then they drove away, and to this day, I have never seen that truck again nor have I seen them in town.

The next day, the Lord called to my mind the name of a salon where I'd worked for a few years. I gave the owner a call and left a message on her answering machine. She returned my call and after we negotiated a deal, she said, "Okay, you can come back and start Friday." Perfect and right on time! God's plan and daily leading unfolded with perfection.

If only in the future, I could stop rushing and pay more attention!

I recalled 2 Corinthians 5:17: *This means that anyone who belongs to Christ has become a new person. The old life is gone; a new life has begun!* Truth: I have seen this verse come to life too many times to list or count.

So there I was, placed through God's provision in a salon with those who had known me before I had completely surrendered my life to Jesus. Now a whole new me was going to be present and God's purpose and work in my heart life and work were going to be unfolding for them to see, not just hear about.

You see, when I had worked there before, I had let anger get the best of me with coworkers who were not especially team oriented. I often found myself caught up in gossip, cursing, etc. Needless to say, the environment was ultra toxic and I actually left the first time because I'd begun a journey with Jesus and felt changes happening inside. That environment was no place for a baby believer still on milk like I was. My wings were still new and I needed a place with less tongue temptation until I learned to rein mine in.

CHAPTER 13

SOARING HIGH

The day I began working at my previous salon again, a newly-licensed lady began working there too. We chatted and discovered we attended the same church. What were the odds? Within a short space of time, the Godcidents that had occurred at my previous salon also began happening on my new job.

For instance, one summer day a seventy-something-year-old woman by the name of Jade arrived for a pedicure. The weather was hot and I'd worn a tank top to work. When I turned around, the client could see I had a tattoo and asked me what it said. I replied, "It's from Isaiah 40:31. *But those who trust in the Lord will find new strength. They will soar high on wings like eagles....*

"You're a Christian?" the lady asked.

"Yes."

She smiled. "I am a new Christian 70+ years old.

I smiled back and said, "It's never too late."

She then shared her amazing testimony about how she came to Christ and who had led her to the feet of Jesus and His Word. She had a dear friend/neighbor for many years who was a Christian. Her neighbor often tried sharing her faith with her. "I always declined," she said. "And responded with unbelief in a God. One day, my neighbor-friend invited me to a barbeque the next day with some of her other friends. I lied. Told her my son was coming to visit and I couldn't attend. My friend never held the barbeque the next day. She passed away that very morning."

I was paying even more attention to Jade's story now.

"My friend had once said, 'I love the Lord so much, I've asked Him — when He is ready — to please take me during worship.' That's exactly what happened. She was in church that morning and she'd kneeled down to pray during a worship song. Never got back up."

"Oh no!" I said.

She continued, "For days I was riddled with guilt. How could my last conversation with a dear friend be a bold-faced lie? I finally felt drawn to walk over and check on her husband. See how he was doing. When I knocked on the door and he appeared, these words flew out of my mouth. 'Can I please have one of my dear friend's Bibles?'

"He replied, 'Of course.' She had several and he gave me one. I walked home and prayed. 'God, please reveal yourself to me.' And He did just that. Leading me to a verse that spoke directly to my situation in life. A verse that applied to that very moment."

Nailed it!

CHAPTER 14

LOVING HOW GOD WORKS

My very last client one evening was Maria, a first-timer at the salon. Though she was very quiet, I tried engaging her in conversation a few times but all I got back were short answers. So I decided to pipe down and work.

I began thinking. Just that week, I'd driven past a sign in front of a church. The sign read T.G.I.F. — Thank God I'm Forgiven. I kept my thoughts to myself and moved on to her pedicure.

Sitting before her, I silently prayed, "Lord, if you want to speak to this woman, go ahead." Momentarily, I heard my text notification on my phone. I took a quick peek and laughed out loud. Another client had just sent me a photo of that exact church sign. I couldn't resist sharing the photo with the woman before me, letting her know I'd seen the sign for real a day or two before. I was thinking, *How funny to have just seen the sign, to be thinking about it now, then get a text with its photo!*

"I live right by that church and I've also seen it," Kimberly said.

That was my cue! So I shared some of my stories, including the story about my husband having lost his job and being provided a new job the same day.

The appointment ended with a deep conversation during which she said that indeed, she needed prayer. Her husband had just lost his job. "Would you pray for me Natalie?" So we prayed.

I simply love how God works!

CHAPTER 15

Don't Miss
the Blessings

My coworker Roe was headed out for the night. She stopped by the pedi room to say goodnight and mentioned to me that a dear client of hers — Karen — had just been diagnosed with cancer. I was well acquainted with Karen and knew she was a sister in Christ. I shared with Roe a bit of a message I'd listened to moments before.

I don't recall the message now, but I remember it being powerful and on time for that moment. It gave me unshakeable faith to pray for Karen. I proclaimed she would have no cancer because I was going to boldly pray. And I did. The next morning I listened to another sermon on healing and faith. I began to ask God to fully lead the day. As I drove to work, a dragonfly flew directly in front of my car. I felt as if he was relaying God's message, "I go before you," from Deuteronomy 1:30: *"The Lord your God is going ahead of you. He will fight for you, just as you saw him do in Egypt."*

The Holy Spirit lead me to call two prayer warrior sisters of mine to come to the salon one day because

Karen was coming in to see me that day. On the way to work, I was prompted to stop at a store to purchase a certain devotional. Walking to the door of the business, I spotted another dragonfly hovering in front of me. *Odd.* Inside making my purchase, I said to the worker, "I am on my way to work and I'm going to be praying over a friend. I'm praying she isn't going to have cancer." I thought my declaration caught him off guard so I chuckled and said, "I'll be back and confirm." It was just one of those on-fire-filled-with-faith kinda days.

Karen didn't yet know that I knew about her diagnosis but as soon as she arrived, I mentioned that I was aware of her cancer diagnosis. I boldly proclaimed, "Not today my friend. We are going to seek God. I have arranged for some sisters to come to help pray. They're on their way."

When the prayer warriors arrived, my friend Cheryl said, "Karen, I've wrapped a gift for you — something I had already made." When Karen unwrapped the gift, she found a beautiful rose with a card with this message: "Karen, God is too wonderful and there are no coincidences in this life."

After our prayer morning, God nailed the answer to that prayer with a big Yes! Karen was declared cancer free. And yes! I drove back to the store where I'd bought the devotional book and shared the story with the same sales clerk I'd promised, "I'll be back with to confirm."

During this entire episode, I'd been thinking about

the woman in Matthew 9:20-22. *Just then a woman who had suffered for twelve years with constant bleeding came up behind him. She touched the fringe of his robe, for she thought, "If I can just touch his robe, I will be healed." Jesus turned around, and when he saw her he said, "Daughter, be encouraged! Your faith has made you well." And the woman was healed at that moment.*

If that woman's faith was so bold that she dared reach for her miracle, my friends and I could claim a miracle over our friend.

You may be wondering what the point is in me sharing all these things. I simply feel that sometimes people think our God is too big and distant. That He is too harsh and cruel. Or that maybe He cannot be approached with everyday concerns. It's the exact opposite. God the creator wants to be deeply connected with His creation.

In every detail of our everyday moments. This astonishing and magnificent God has become such a huge part of every moment in my day that I feel I cannot breathe without Him. I love how He cares for me and makes His presence known.

For instance, one day I told my husband I would love to make at least $100 to buy some pants. That Saturday, a client I hadn't seen in a long time messaged me asking if I could see her sister that day for a mani/pedi. "And can you please extend my price?"

"Of course!"

When they came in, she and her sister and I had a dynamite conversation about Jesus and how He was working in our lives. Visiting from Africa, my client shared about the interesting work God had allowed her to be a part of. At the end of the appointment I distinctly felt that God was telling me not to charge her a penny for the services. I thought, *Really Lord? I would get at least $45 and now, zero. Oh, my.* I knew He was clearly talking to me so I obeyed. As the two ladies walked out, my friend turned around and said, "Can I tip you?"

I couldn't help but laugh. "Is this a trick question? I suppose that's up to you." Placing a tip in my top drawer, she left with her sister. At the end of the day I opened the drawer to find a one hundred dollar bill.

I sat back and gave the tip some thought. If I hadn't obeyed the Lord, I would have settled for less. Less of what God has is less of His promises, less of the opportunity for another testimony of His majesty. We often settle for less and miss out on so many opportunities He has laid out for us when we do. We can miss out on blessings because in Deuteronomy 28:1-14, God's word definitely mentions we can be blessed in "Blessings for Obedience."

I don't obey for monetary gain or for self glory. I obey for no other reason than the Glory of God alone.

I want to boast in nothing other than I know and understand the Lord. Take a look at Jeremiah 9:22-24 when you get a chance.

Glory to you God Holy, Holy, Holy, are you Lord Almighty.

My hope and my prayer is maybe, just maybe, my readers will take a look at those verses just mentioned and read deeper. Maybe you'll pray a crazy prayer and Adonai, our Lord, will answer. Maybe you'll mention one story to someone and they will share their story with you.

I have no idea what's in store after writing out these stories from my life chapter by chapter, but I know the One who created these stories to take place by aligning my appointments to make paths cross so events would occur. He created and designed them all.

CHAPTER 16

GOD NUDGES

I have two more hundred-dollar-bill experiences. One dates way back when I was not following Jesus. Perhaps it was one of God's first nudges my way? I'll let you decide.

My daughters were very small and I was a stay-at-home mom. One morning I discovered a water bill was due that day. The bill was exactly $100 and the water would be shut off by seven P.M. if it wasn't paid. I was so stressed, my nerves stretched to the breaking point. As my girls played in the living room, I sat on my bed with tears spilling down my face.

I didn't want to ask my parents for help. My husband was working hard (as he has always done and still does), but I didn't want to bother him with problems. Something deep down made me say a small prayer. I don't recall words, but I clearly remember not being able to squeeze out one more tear.

After cleaning up in the bathroom, I began doing laundry. A load of the kids' clothes had just finished. As I transferred the load to the dryer, a $100 bill fell out.

I have not made this up. I kid you not. There is no way it belonged to my husband. With no experience of God and His goodness, I didn't know that God had nailed it without my even realizing it was a special gift from Him. However, that small prayer was answered to the penny.

Years later, when my oldest child was in high school, a friend of hers who lived around the corner with her single mom, Lauren, had the same experience. Here's how her Godcident happened: One night Lauren came over and knocked on my door. Once inside, she asked, "Did your daughter mention anything about what happened last night?"

"No, she didn't," I replied. And her story spilled out.

"We owed $55 on a water bill by 7 P.M." I was thinking, *Seven P.M.? Wait a minute. This sounds familiar. But this woman has no idea what happened to me....*

Lauren continued, "I was stressed about the bill — How would I pay it? — and went into my bedroom where I began reading my Bible. Then I started my laundry."

Are you kidding me with the laundry? Come on! Laundry?

"In the first load of clothes, I found $20."

Yes!

"I washed a few more loads, and couldn't believe it. In those other loads of clothes more money washed out. Exactly $50, and not one penny more."

My neighbor was experiencing such joy and wonderment, and I was lapping up every word coming out of her mouth. Simply ahhhh-mazing! Perhaps God was trying to tell both of us something. *"Yeah, it's ME, and I'm here looking after you two. When are you going to come to me?* Perhaps those were some of his first nudges for me to acknowledge Him.

CHAPTER 17

DON'T WORRY
ABOUT TOMORROW

The next $100 bill story is one of pure awe and grace.
My daughter's eighth grade prom was coming
up. Money was tight as always with our call in life. My
husband had asked me to save $100 from my paycheck
for her dinner that following Friday.

First, Monday came and she needed a dress and
shoes. After making those purchases, I was down to
what seemed like chump change.

Next, she came home and mentioned she wanted to
wear a dress that her cousin let her borrow. Inside, I was
happy about that arrangement thinking, *Perfect, I can
return the other dress and have at least $50.*

The following day I drove to the automatic teller
machine (ATM) because my bank statement said I
had exactly $100 in the account. Inside, however, the
Holy Spirit was whispering, *Only $50 of that amount is
yours.* I didn't listen. I thought, *I'll just pay fees later,* and
against my better judgment, I withdrew the entire $100.

The following day, I received a text from Bailey,
a friend who had moved to Oklahoma. When she'd

lived by me, I'd shared many of these stories and other testimonies with her. Bailey often wrestled with her faith because of unanswered prayers. (Believe me, I also wrestle with unanswered prayer and still do but I have to go back and remind myself of all the answered prayer.) Her text read, "Call me when you can."

So, I called her on my way home. Bailey was filled with energy. She told me about how she had been attending church. Then, "I've been feeling the presence of God and I want to start giving back. I told God, 'I don't have much and I'm a single mom on unemployment but I'm going to faithfully tithe $20.'

"There I was at church one Sunday with $27 to my name for the whole week. Natalie, somehow I had this newfound trust I can't explain; but with my whole heart, I gave the $20. The next day, I needed milk and eggs and knew all I had was $7. I decided to drive through the ATM to make sure the $7 was still there. You'll have a hard time believing this but my ATM balance read that I had hundreds available. Baffled, I went into the bank and after much examination of my bank records, the banker said, 'Ma'am, it's your money.'

"I said, 'That's impossible.' So the banker printed out a statement for me. Come to find out, the money *was* my money. And here's why: I'd never received a penny from my daughter's father. As matter of fact, he'd never really held a job. But by the grace of God, there it was on that bank statement and from out of nowhere…a child support payment. Praise you, Lord!"

After her enthusiastic testimony, I gave a huge sigh and (with all seriousness) said, "Well, this sucks." Not the best language, I know, but I'm being honest here and laying it bare. That's what blurted out of my mouth because I was so disappointed in myself.

Of course, my friend was confused. I laughed and told her, "I tried to tell you so many times about this big God. Well, guess what girl? I am now sitting here at my bank and I know I have to put $50 back and Trust God."

I did just that.

That night a friend, who was also my hairdresser and client, messaged me asking to purchase a gift card for her sister. She didn't say when she wanted it or anything, she just asked, "How much?" I replied, "Fifty bucks."

The night before prom she messaged me again. This time she asked to swing by on her way out of town the next day; she had broken a nail. "Come by early," I said.

On prom day I barely had any money left. After I fixed my friend's nail, she placed a $100 bill on my sink. She mentioned buying the gift card and I said, "Okay, but I have no change."

She smiled and said, "No. It's all for you for always taking care of my nails."

The time eventually came when I shared with her about being an answer to prayer that day!

If I had given into temptation and taken the extra fifty out of my account — the fifty that would have made my account overdrawn — and not trusted or sought God, I wouldn't have had this Godcident story to tell. Or any God stories for that matter.

Jesus declared in Matthew 6:24-25, *"No one can serve two masters. For you will hate one and love the other; you will be devoted to one and despise the other. You cannot serve God and be enslaved to money. That is why I tell you not to worry about everyday life – whether you have enough food and drink, or enough clothes to wear. Isn't life more than food, and your body more than clothing?"*

He went on to say instead of worrying about everyday things we should seek the kingdom of God and His righteousness first and God will give us everything we need.

So don't worry about tomorrow.... (v 34).

I was beginning to catch on.

Over the last ten-plus years, I have seen this promise fulfilled over and over again. Now I live minute by minute and day by day relying on Him. Some days I falter but he brings me back to His word and all He has done to remind me. He often has me sit at a nail station and repeatedly share testimony after testimony all the while I'm also using them to remind *myself* of his graciousness, mercy, and provision. This God who calls himself Yahweh — I Am — is worthy of adoration. There are no words to describe how it felt when I finally realized these truths.

CHAPTER 18

THE ENVELOPE THEORY

One day while at the salon, I told a co-worker — Allison — about the time I was driving to my daughter's cheer class. "It was late. While I drove, I spoke with God in the silence. 'God, there's this verse that says delight yourself in the Lord and He will give you the desires of your heart. (Psalm 37:4) So, you know God, I would like a white BMW. I don't think that's too much to ask. I am over money. And I don't need a big house. So yeah, a BMW sounds good.'

"Well, it felt as if He sat right next to me and I heard in my heart, clear as day as if I were standing here face to face with you: "Is that what you would ask for if you met me face to face?" I was overcome with tears and replied, 'Absolutely not. I would ask for my dad to believe in you.' You see, He revealed to me what the true desire in my heart really was. And my true desire wasn't the temporary wants of the world."

Allison laughed and said, "Well, do you care the year or color of the BMW?" Her comment was so random and off the wall that I burst out laughing and replied, "Not really. Just a certain style I guess."

She shot back, "You will have it girl!"

I laughed again. And thought no more about my wishful thinking.

Fast forward a few months. I was taking my oldest out to breakfast and calling for my middle child to join us. She kept refusing, "Mom, I'm asleep!"

"Okay, we will grab you after."

I picked up my oldest from her friend's and we left to go eat. While we were at the restaurant, my daughter realized she'd forgotten her retainer and we needed to go back to her friend's house. We were stopped at the intersection waiting to turn onto the street where her friend lived when I heard the squeal of tires. The sound seemed to be coming from my left. As I glanced to the left, a big bump from behind shoved my car through the intersection! A man had crashed directly into the vehicle stopped behind me causing the poor man behind me to smash into me, crushing in the trunk of my car so much it was about half the size it should have been. I was thankful my other daughter hadn't come because she might have been injured in the back seat.

Well, my car was totaled. The next day, when I attempted to drive our other car to take the kids to school *it* started making a loud sound. My brother-in-law came out and looked underneath the car. He discovered that someone had used a blowtorch and had stolen our catalytic converters. *Are you kidding me?!* Such a hard week.

Now, I had no car myself, and an estimate of approximately $1,300 to repair our second car.

But God....

Love that statement.

On my most desperate day God showed up right on time with a rental paid for by the insurance company. Then they gave us a payout check for around $5,000. I used some of the money to immediately fix our second vehicle. I then drove...and prayed for the Almighty to lead me to a car that would cost around no more than what I had left, $3,500. This little thought popped into my head. *Call your aunt.* For a long time, she'd kept a car that didn't run in her garage. *Wasn't it a BMW, if it's still the same one?* I messaged her. She still had it so we decided to tow the car to a repair shop and have it checked out. To my surprise, my aunt's car was the exact style of BMW I loved.

I. Could. Not. Believe. It.

Repairing the car would cost an estimated $500. I offered my aunt and uncle the three thousand I had left and they accepted. My uncle said, "Jesus said to only take what you have and bless you with the car."

The BMW was now mine. And here's my favorite part: The morning I was to pick up the BMW, I checked my bank account. I had an unexplained two hundred dollar deposit from a nail site that had closed a while back. I phoned the company because I figured a mistake had been made. After some research the woman on the line assured me the money was mine and owed to me. I was so excited! I thought, *Ha! I'm gonna go buy some shoes! I love shoes!*

But in the automotive repair office with the mechanic and another gentleman, the mechanic said, "I quoted you $500 for the repair, however, the car needs another part that will cost $200."

Friends, I kid you not, I quickly opened my bank statement to show the men and to "declare the Lord's glory and provision."

Hallelujah!

Showing the men the recent deposit, I declared, "Jesus knew I would need that money today!" After the mechanic left for my car the other gentleman said, "Did that really happen the way you said it did?"

With a big grin I replied, "Yes, and it always does."

Then I shared this with him: "A few years ago I heard a sermon from a pastor I admire who preaches in Rocklin. He started the message with, 'Church, today some of you are not going to be happy with what the Lord has for me to say. Some of you will never, ever, achieve a savings account or money past a day in this lifetime. That is because God is training you to be like the Israelites when He provided manna.' (He was referring to the heart-wrenching but incredible story of God's provision for the Israelites in the 40-year desert wandering — part of their history after being freed from slavery in Egypt.) The pastor continued, 'In the desert, God told the people He would provide manna — a sweet kind of flaky substance they gathered that would make bread. God told the Israelites to take only what they needed for their family for one day and not to take extra and try to store it because it would rot. That is exactly what happened, because like us, some didn't fully believe God, even when seeing miracles. The point was, God was testing His people in the desert. Testing them to see if they believed He would provide for them.'

"As soon as I heard this message, I knew that preacher was talking to me. The sermon was actually funny because he asked his congregation, 'Have any of you ever tried the envelope theory?' I couldn't keep from laughing because I had tried this experiment after a friend invited me to a Financial Peace class at her church. Here's how it works: Make envelopes labeled with every penny to be spent for owed bills and then label one as a "savings" envelope. I'll tell you right now that God wouldn't provide a penny more for me if I had even $5 in that savings envelope. So yes, I was very familiar with the envelope theory…and that's how I knew the pastor was talking directly to me.

I was one of those people who had been tested my entire life to build my faith in God when it came to His daily provision for me. I had to surmise a savings account wasn't written into my destiny plan. So I looked at this guy in the automotive repair shop and said, "That pastor was describing my life. But look at God — He has never failed me. Ever. In any and all of my needs. I could write a book on nothing but God's provision." And I was thinking how wonderful it was to share stories with this gentleman.

He looked at me and said, "You know, I think that this is my scenario too." Though I knew I'd never see him again, I prayed he would seek and find God.

My BMW acquisition was proof for me that Psalm 37:4 — *Take delight in the Lord, and he will give you your heart's desires.* — was reliable and true.

Even if God were to say *no* to a prayer — for instance, even if both of my cars had been non-operational and I'd never laid hands on the BMW — there has to be a good reason for a *no*, because God is all knowing and Sovereign. He knows what's best for me. If He alone is my delight, and His way and purpose is first in my heart, that's what the Father and the Son are after.

In my relationship with Jesus I've come to realize God is after hearts, not works. Not performance — who owns the most toys. And certainly not perfection, rules, or regulations. We'd all fail miserably if those things were what He was after.

Hebrews 12:1-2 tells us: *Let us strip off every weight that slows us down, especially the sin that so easily trips us up. And let us run with endurance the race God has set before us. We do this by keeping our eyes on Jesus, the champion who initiates and perfects our faith. Because of the joy awaiting him, he endured the CROSS* [emphasis mine], *disregarding its shame. Now he is seated in the place of honor beside God's throne.*

Jesus took all our sin so that we can be reconciled to a holy, just God. You see, we are not holy and we are not good, but God is. He is so good that when He created us in the beginning, everything was perfect. Genesis 1:26-31 is a record of the creation. My favorite part is verse 31: *Then God said, "Let us make human beings in our image, to be like us. They will reign over the fish in the sea, the birds in the sky, the livestock, all the wild animals on earth, and the small animals that scurry along the ground....And God looked over all he had made, and he saw that it was VERY GOOD!"* [emphasis mine] The problem was, God gave His creation free will to choose to walk in unity with Him.

Man fell because of pride, lust, and selfishness. God did not create robots but humans with free will, He commanded them to tend the earth, multiply, and not to eat from one tree. Eve was tempted because she saw that it *looked good.* (Isn't it always because we are filled with wanting to satisfy our own will and lusts!) That one act of sin created separation from man and God.

CHAPTER 19

PROVISION

I'd like to share one more amazing example of God's great love and mercy. Genesis 3:4-21 is the whole picture; however, from the beginning God has clearly stated that justice is due when man goes his own selfish way. Here it is. Take your time to carefully read it.

The Lord God made clothing from animal skins for Adam and his wife. Then the Lord God said, "Look, the human beings have become like us, knowing both good and evil. What if they reach out, take fruit from the tree of life, and eat it? Then they will live forever!" So the Lord God banished them from the Garden of Eden, and he sent Adam out to cultivate the ground from which he had been made. After sending them out, the Lord God stationed mighty cherubim to the east of the Garden of Eden. And he placed a flaming sword that flashed back and forth to guard the way to the tree of life. (Genesis 3:21-24)

Do you see it? After all their disobedience, God still clothed them beautifully. And Jesus has become our righteousness given to us as a gift.

The sin of this one man, Adam, caused death to rule over many. But even greater is God's wonderful grace and his gift of righteousness, for all who receive it will live in triumph over sin and death through this one man, Jesus Christ. (Romans 5:17)

When we are covered by Jesus' blood, God looks down and sees us covered with that beautiful free gift of love.

This is why He is my delight. He is my Joy. He is my peace in all storms. He is my provider. He is my all.

So, back to the subject of the BMW. I'm sharing this story over and over with so many clients. I was driving home one day and boom! Flat tire. UGH!

I pulled over onto a side street and examined the situation. A man down the street yelled, "Need any help changing that flat?"

"Yes! The jack is too hard to figure out!" I yelled back.

The man, Darren, brought his own jack and came to the rescue. Afterwards, he made the funniest statement. "I helped because I own a BMW, too." Then he laughed real big like I didn't have anything on him. I replied, "Ha-ha! That's cool." But then with a sly grin I added, "Jesus gave me this one."

Darren stopped what he was doing and gave me a yeah-right look. But then he said, "Well, *I* was at a crab feed and the woman next to me was excited about her new BMW; she looked at me and said, 'Do you need a car?' I told her 'Well, yeah!' and she said, 'Okay, you can have my old BMW.'"

Yep. You read that right. He received a free BMW from a total stranger. Guess he topped my story.

But I couldn't help but get in the last word and said, "Hey, I believe Jesus might have arranged this flat tire here to tell you that the BMW you got from that lady — was really from Him."

As I wander through each day with my eyes fixed on Him, these very moments turn into opportunities He uses to strike up conversations with my clients, friends, family, and strangers.

Vicki has her own story about God giving one of His loved ones the desires of her heart.

While working on this book with Natalie, I took a break and walked to the kitchen for a snack. On the way there, I thought, *It sure would be nice to fly back out to Danville to see Natalie again so we could talk about the book, make edits without using email, and just chat, catch up, and take a few selfies together for promotional shots. But a flight to Danville, just for a short visit, would be expensive. Guess that's not happening any time soon.*

A couple of hours later, after I'd blown the Cheetos dust off my laptop and tried to stop thinking about those fudge brownies in the kitchen, my daughter called.

"Hi Mom. We're thinking about flying out to Hawaii for Thanksgiving with the In-Love's at their beach house. We'll be stopping over at their home in California for a short break before leaving for the islands the next day. We're flying first class with the kids thanks to their generosity and free tickets. And your ticket is paid for too. Want to come?"

Oh God, you are so good! Nailed that one for sure.

That was another time when I hadn't even prayed for that vacation, it had only been a nice thought — a nice bucket-list wish, and God had been delighted to give me the desires of my heart through the generosity of extended family. And to get in a possible visit with Natalie to boot? What a mighty God I serve!

CHAPTER 20

BE STILL AND KNOW

I believe God took me back to a certain salon to meet Allison. She once led me on an amazing adventure. While working together God actually used her in one of the toughest spots I was in at the time.

Around October 2012, the year before the BMW, my husband lost his job for a second time. As matter of fact, we had to move out of our four bedroom townhouse on New Year's Eve. The reason I mention the size of the townhouse is because our family of five moved to a two-bedroom/one-bathroom home…with another relative, her husband, and three dogs.

I love to tell people 2013 was the hardest and best year of my life. There were days when I could easily feel ungrateful and sorry for myself. God never left me though. He actually grew my faith and love for Him. Each time I thought I had reached the end of my rope, He swooped in with rest and retreat.

For instance, one day at work Allison came to my desk not knowing the state of my emotions that day. She asked if I could take off for the weekend and attend a women's retreat with her. I told her I would love to but I couldn't afford it. She said I could attend for free because other women donated. Praise you God for your faithful on-time love, and right before this retreat, which was in October — my birthday month. God is too good!

We had planned to hang out together on my actual birthday, a time that would include breakfast, going on a hike, and probably consignment store shopping. The night before my birthday, while heading to bed, I told my husband my plans. "Those are the plans, and you know what, I believe I have discovered the best verse in the whole Bible!"

He said, "That's a big book with a lot in there."

I said, "Yes, but somewhere — I have no idea where — there is a verse that says, 'Be still and know that I AM GOD.' And if our tiny minds could wrap around this truth, and trust that He truly is in control, we could actually have rest."

So the very next day I headed to my friend's house, never having shared with her about that verse. As we prepared to leave her house she said, "First, I have a gift for you."

Opening the package, I found a beautiful coffee cup with the words "BE STILL & KNOW I AM GOD — PSALM 46:10." Amazing, I tell you. Only then did I know where those wonderful words could be found in the Bible.

The next weekend was our retreat and it so happened that the place we were going was my favorite summer destination. We arrived at this pristine setting in the mountains, taking in the clean air, and were soon joined by awesome women.

Enjoying delicious food and fellowship, we were also blessed with an awesome guest speaker. One night the speaker was sitting in the back of the room so I sat down beside her to "pick" her heart and brain. I said, "How do I do this? How do I get on a stage to tell women how amazing a life with Jesus is?"

She gave me the most beautiful response. "Don't covet that stage. A lot comes with it. Let God lead and use you where you are, only then are you ready." She paused for a second, then she continued, "Natalie, be still and know He is God."

I honestly couldn't believe my ears. I ran out and found Allison to tell her what had just happened. The speaker was telling me that when God speaks, He makes a "calling" very clear. And the same words are usually repeated from someone else, and always align with His word and truth.

CHAPTER 21

THE SUPER HERO

What's so cool about the encounter with Allison is that almost exactly to the date of the previous October, the same thing happened to me. During the time of my husband's job loss, I had become so overwhelmed that I drove to Home Depot and sat there looking around in desperation. "God, please give me two days off in this life I'm living, for free. Thanks." That was it. Simple. To the point. And He heard my cry.

That Sunday morning I planned on attending my church service at 11 A.M. As I was combing my hair, this small, inside voice whispered, "Go to Christa's church today."

I thought, *No way. I'll never make it. That service starts in like, twenty minutes. I have three teens that will never be ready on time.* So I tried to ignore that prompting; but it came again. So I said, "Okay God." Then ran down the hall and told them to be ready in ten minutes. We made it five minutes after start time. Whew!

As I sat through the sermon I thought, *Hmmmmm. This doesn't seem like a direct message to me.* Afterward I mingled with some of the awesome women I had met before. One of them asked me if I was attending the women's retreat the following weekend. My reply was, "No, until today I had no idea there was a retreat next weekend. Besides, I can't afford it."

Christa had mentioned it was sold out, but a few days later, she texted me and asked a question I would come to hear often. "Natalie, can you take two days off this weekend?"

I told her I could move some clients and make it work but what was the occasion? Her reply was the very reason I had been led to the church service. "There is a spot open at the retreat and a woman paid for you to come." It is often when I am at the end of my rope that God shows up to be the true super hero that He is.

CHAPTER 22

OPENED DOORS

One day May 2013, while driving to the salon, I prayed with all my heart, "God, what is my purpose?" I heard in my heart, "Teens and youth." I thought, *Okay, I have three teens so maybe my purpose is to teach them and their friends.* Which is a Yes! But He had more. Soon after that prayer a regular client invited me to attend a women's event at her church. I invited my cousin, Stephanie, to go with me. That day changed my life once again. I learned God has many purposes for us — we are to just listen as He leads.

This was such a lovely event filled with hundreds of women, yummy breakfasts, lots of coffee and several speakers. One of the speakers was a young lady named Wendy. She stood on the stage with a teenage girl, Alice, to talk about a ministry called Young Life. Alice gave her testimony of how a friend in school had invited her to a youth camp for a week in summer. Alice had gladly accepted with, "Yes! A week away from my parents, ha!" Alice had no idea she would meet Jesus and He would change the course of her life.

Wendy then shared how God had brought her to this town because God was calling her to start a Young

Life ministry there, actually at the very high school my daughters attended. My heart raced! I knew the Holy Spirit was telling me to *listen up*.

Wendy finished and left the front of the room to return to her seat. I was so enthralled with the next speaker who walked on the stage I lost track of her. The speaker said, "I feel led to pray over Wendy and for this new ministry." As she prayed she said words that pierced my soul: "Someone is here today because God has brought you to be part of this." I knew it was me she was speaking to and tears flowed down my cheeks because His presence was overwhelming. Honestly, when the woman who spoke after Wendy prayed, I wanted to leap up before everyone and say, "Stop! It's me! You're praying for me!" I looked at my cousin and shared with her what was happening inside me. I then took out a business card and wrote a little about myself on the back and told Stephanie I had to meet Wendy after the session.

Little did I know that in a few minutes, in this huge room filled with people, I would slightly maneuver my chair around and find Wendy sitting right next to me. She'd been there the entire time. I introduced myself and handed her my business card. She read it. Then her expression showed she was stunned. When she turned it over to my business side she asked, "Do you know a woman at church named Lisa?" I'm usually terrible with names but I did remember Lisa. I said, "I met her only once; a year ago by way of a nail coupon. She did ministry work in Africa."

"Yes!" Wendy said. "That's her. Lisa approached me at church and said she'd met a manicurist in that city who I should meet to do ministry with."

"Come on, are you kidding me?" *God you are so mighty and big and so close at the same time. How could a random "universe" come up with an introduction like this?*

A few weeks later Wendy and I met for coffee. I was all in for whatever God had planned. The meeting ended with an invitation to a leader retreat coming up at some woman's cabin — a woman I'd never met. I must say, before all of this I would never go to an event where I didn't know people. I was very much a keep-me-in-my-circle kind of girl who didn't like any kind of adventure. But now, I left my comfort zone and showed up at the home of a woman by the name of Jane, expecting all of the leaders to be my age. How wrong I was. I felt like I was at camp because everyone was college age and younger! A young woman named Jane ran over to me as if she'd known me for years and said, "Several leaders will be riding in your car." She led the leaders with their suitcases to my vehicle. I found myself driving loud youngsters to a stranger's cabin. I was freaked out.

When we pulled over for a coffee break, I ran to the bathroom and called my best friend, Leanne. I said, "Girl,

God is trippin! He has me with all these young strangers. I think I'm gonna leave them here and go home."

"No!" she said. "You go. It's going to be amazing."

When we arrived at the cabin, everyone seemed to know each other, and have routines that included board games, card games, instruments being played and coffee served along with hot cocoa. Placing my bags by a bed, I sat down, feeling out of place because everyone was so much younger. But later we gathered for the meeting and I saw that a few other adults had arrived. "Thank you Lord, really."

We relaxed some and before the meeting the youth gathered their instruments and began to play worship songs. I sat there with tear filled eyes. (I clearly feel the same emotion as I write this.) *Wow, oh wow!* I thought. *Some kid invited these kids to a camp that changed their lives one summer and now here they are, wanting to be leaders who bring other kids to a Young Life camp. God thank you for letting me see and be part of your plan.*

The next day was the funniest. Jane mentioned that we had an "adventure" planned that afternoon and to wear a swimsuit. *Yeah! No way! And around those youngsters? I'll pass thanks.*

I approached Jane and asked if I could be filled in on what this "adventure" would entail. She said, "We usually don't tell. That's why it's an adventure." I assured her I was not very adventurous. She had pity on me.

Yes! She shared what the details were and I "nicely" declined. "I'll keep watch!"

So, I (and a few others) refrained from going. That's when I met Allen, one of the main committee members. I shared my testimony about how I ended up at that cabin. The moment was so spirit filled, Allen couldn't hold back tears as he shared how the committee had been praying for years that God would lead someone to start a Young Life in that very city where I lived.

Well, there I was with the others led by God for the adventure of a lifetime.

Throughout the year God gently stretched me. The process was truly something wonderful. My transformation changed my life one step at a time. I met some of the most amazing kiddos and leaders and had amazing "adventures."

On one such adventure, a winter retreat for some youth in Tahoe, I found myself sleeping, and sharing a bathroom, with approximately 75 teen girls. These girls were Godsends filled with stories of life, hard times, and Jesus leading them. (Again, writing this right now is filling me with tears and joy all at the same time. To go back in my mind and having the Holy Spirit reminding me is filling my soul.)

"Adventure" morning arrived. This time I was "in" and had no idea what was ahead. Hopping into cars, we drove until we finally arrived at Donner Summit. Okay, yes, it's a mountain. However, I wore sneakers to hike up this mountain that was still swaddled in patches of snow.

The front of the mountain is tall and majestic. All uphill — frightening with skinny switchbacks to negotiate. The teens, including my daughters, flew up while I lagged below, struggling with fear. (Did I mention I have a fear of heights?) As my shoe often slid on icy ground I looked up and thought, *These leaders have lost their minds.*

Kyle — Allison's son — and I slowly made our way. Kyle was sick; and no question about it, I was terrified. Around the middle of this trek, I stopped. All of the kids and leaders looked down chanting, "Mama Nat, you can do it!" Um. No, I really couldn't.

So Jane's husband, Dan, retraced his steps to me. Taking my hand, he sweetly said, "Come on." With as much conviction as I could muster I said, "No Dan. Really. I'll wait here and spend time with Jesus." But Dan's confidence was reassuring and I accepted his offer to hike with me.

And I made it!

As I rounded a bend near the top, I came full face with breathtaking scenery that overwhelmed me. Blankets of snow were visible, and as I walked for miles with Dan's help, I made it to the top of the summit where the view of the lake looked like a travel photograph. Making my way back down, I could not believe I'd actually survived the strenuous hike. By then, the sun was setting. One of the young guy leaders yelled at me. "Slow down! You're missing the most awesome sunset." I reassured him. "It's okay. My main focus is to make it down the hill before sunlight is gone!"

The next morning while the kids cooked breakfast and we all gathered to listen to the speakers, Jesus whispered to me. "Natalie, I took you up that mountain because that will be your life. You won't know what's around the corner but I will be with you."

CHAPTER 23

TRANSFORMATION

F ast-forward a bit to summer of 2013. Some people are brought into our lives for a short season and reason. Allison was one of those. One day she invited me to join her sister's family business making pizza at a carnival in Oregon. Allison explained: "We will be glamping in tents with all the other carnival people." I had never ever done anything quite like that and thought it was a crazy idea.

This new adventure was far out of my comfort zone, but I prayed. God said go, and when He says go, I want my response to be a 'yes' without hesitation. This would be one of those mountains I'd need to tackle.

So, Allison and I were off to Oregon in her new SUV, and since I loved pizza that worked for me. We arrived to find the tents were very cool. Her sister had ours looking like a Hilton, even with cots and mattresses. Mornings found us eating early, then getting ready to cook and serve fresh pizza all day. I walked by cows and all sorts of animals and, go figure — the name of the carnival was "God Made a Farmer."

One day, I shared about Young Life and Young Lives with Allison's sister and she told me she had been a Young

Life leader. I thought, *God, how cool. Here you are again. Always everywhere. Ready to keep me going.* The next morning Allison's sister wanted to tell me something. She said, "I was just in my tent and God gave me a scripture to share with you. James 3:5: *The tongue is a little member, and boasteth great things. Behold, how great a matter a little fire kindleth!*" God truly sent me on this little adventure to reassure this was His plan for me.

On our drive home I felt compelled to share a story with a woman I had met at Christa's church. It was something that had happened on one of my visits to her church a few years earlier.

We were sitting in the back row and during worship and my favorite song began: "How Great Is Our God." As I started to sing (not one of my gifts) I felt a fiery sensation all around me. The only way I know to describe it would be to say it was like only the Spirit of God and I were present at that moment.

During the sermon a young man from the back row walked up and knelt down next to Christa. In my mind I was thinking, *What is this guy doing? This is so rude because the pastor is speaking.* Once the message ended Christa walked onto the platform and asked everyone to stay seated. She told the church, "A young man just approached me with a message for someone and he'd like to share the message." When she turned the meeting over to him, the young man said, "The Lord gave me a vision for someone." And he proceeded to point at me! I thought, *No way. I don't even know you.* I wasn't accustomed to anything like this happening during worship.

Then he said, "Could you and your husband please come to the platform." I figured my husband was probably thinking, *Oh, great! What kind of place and event has my wife brought me to?* As we approached the speakers, the young man I'd thought had been so rude said, "While we were singing I saw fire all around you. The Lord said your words will be like fire. That your purpose is to bring the next generation of teens to Jesus."

And look where I was years later! With teens! I had to share with that woman — the young man's mom, who by divine appointment was in the same car with me on the ride home — that those words were unfolding into a life I could never have imagined. A life where God was giving and taking away because He wanted to set me free. Free from false hope in false idols like money, material items, houses, jobs, careers, kids...you name it.

God's people make these things idols — objects of worship and His people place their importance over Him and then have the audacity to wonder where He is. God is actually very present and available. Yet those He created have a clouded vision and have set preconceived notions and thoughts on and about God. If His children really sought Him out, along with His truth, we might consider that He is not looking to fill us with information but with transformation. He will reveal Himself as a loving Father, an amazing Creator, a caring and selfless Savior, a never-ending pursuer of our souls. It's true. All of it. And He will open the eyes of those who seek and ask.

I know this from personal experience. You see, once I was at the salon where He started to speak daily, He asked me to choose Him.

CHAPTER 24

BELIEVING
WHAT WE BELIEVE

In September of 2013, Wendy invited my girls and me on a Young Life rafting trip. My husband and I already had reservations at a timeshare in Tahoe that weekend so Wendy said, "I'll gladly take your girls on the trip."

The night before the trip, I dropped off my girls and headed to the bank to deposit my paycheck. We needed my check for the trip because my husband's payday wasn't until the following week. I drove to the drive-through ATM and checked my balance. After I made the deposit, the screen suddenly turned black. When the screen once again appeared, my balance read zero. I hesitated to retrieve my card, but I finally did and then ran into the bank.

After a few nail-biting minutes, the teller explained that the entire system had been hit with a virus. I would have to wait until Monday to talk to someone. I couldn't believe it! No money. So, no way could we go to Tahoe. I explained to my husband, then said, "I guess this is God's way of saying no. He must have a plan. So the

153

next day I went on the rafting trip. And surprisingly enough, after we cancelled the trip to Tahoe, my money became available the next day. I truly believe that God has a sense of humor!

A few days later, on September 17th, I had the day off. Or so I thought.

I dropped my girls off at school and then my coworker asked me to take her son to school so I drove to pick him up and took him to school.

That same day, someone's Facebook (FB) post read "we must truly believe *what we believe.*" I couldn't agree more.

If I truly believe God has a plan for each day, then I should be flexible and open to His plan, not mine. Often I try to make plans and they go in an entirely different direction. But on those days, events happen for someone to encounter Him.

On this particular day that's what happened. After I dropped off my coworker's son, I received a friend request on FB from a well known pastor. Of course the FB friend request was from a hacked or cloned account but the cool part is the request message was Phillipians 4:6: *Be careful for nothing; but in everything by prayer and supplication with thanksgiving let your requests be made known unto God.*

I soon got a call for a nail appointment so I went to work since I had the time to accommodate her. Shortly after the woman arrived, I was telling her about my fake friend request — who it was and the Bible verse on the FB wall. I also told her about the borrowing-from-my-account incident when I didn't have the money, and trying to force my own way and plans instead of waiting for God's plans for me.

She was so funny; she just kept repeating, "Only God."

And she was right. Only God could speak to his children, rearrange our day, and show up for us through situations and people.

God doesn't just show up to comfort and guide. He also shows up as a loving Father with correction.

In the middle of all that was going on that summer my husband and I went to a Bible study one Wednesday night at the church our family attended. It was crazy what I heard. The pastor kept saying, "God gives and takes away. God gives and takes away." There seemed to be an echo in the deepest part of my heart. I knew God was growing something in me and teaching me a new thing.

My husband and I walked out of Bible study that night and I said, "It's my fault. Sometimes we take God's gifts for granted and we complain about them. Back when we received the answer to prayer about the townhouse in Dublin, when God provided the exact place I had prayed for, I became unhappy and wanted more. Instead of being content I became a complainer. Instead of being grateful, I was bitter. I was constantly looking for a bigger place. Or a nicer backyard. I was always searching for more, and God gave that so then I realized He also took it away."

This revelation was as clear as day. I mean, if I put myself in God's shoes — which I should never do — I'd find out just how small and minute I am.

Trying to get my head into God's way of thinking, I then realized, I, too, would want to take something away from someone who only complained and was never thankful. Right? Very true. God was extremely just in disciplining and taking away. Teaching me to be thankful even for a place less than half the size in the years to come. I'm still on that journey as I write this today. Oh, but a new thing has begun. You'll see.

Some days it's hard to feel the presence of God, hear Him or see Him at work. I was having a day like that when I decided to pray for His presence. I remember praying, *God show up today, let me see you today.*

I dropped my daughter off at softball and decided to go to a nearby gas station to wash my car with my youngest. As I drove out of the car wash, I pulled over to dry the car off. Next to me was an area with trash cans. A very sick little boy was there with his dad, John.

As I came around the front of my car John asked if I had any recommendations. I replied, "I would try Gatorade and crackers."

I then felt a nudge from the Holy Spirit. Though I

was hesitant, I decided to go for it. I turned and said, "I could pray for him."

Seemingly confused, John said, "What?"

I said, "We could pray over him, if that's okay." John replied, "Yes. Yes, it is." So there I was at a gas station, walking over to John and his child to pray.

We prayed for God to heal this little guy. John looked up, introduced himself and asked my name and what church I attended. I told him. And John said, "My good friend is the pastor of that church. It's awesome to see someone living out church."

I was humbled that God had actually answered my prayer. After I had dried off my car and was preparing to leave, John waved me down. The father and child had begun to walk home and John said, "My son feels better." With a joyful laugh he said, "God is too good."

Yes He is. God really sees us and wants to pour out hope and love. He will use anyone or anything if our eyes and hearts are open and responsive.

CHAPTER 25

Providing a Well

So many times in the beginning of my walk with God, He would present an event to attend, the invitation often requiring a last minute decision. I had to make a choice. Did I go and cancel the client who paid me the most, knowing if I canceled her appointment, she would most likely never return?

Over and over again I made the decision to choose Him, and the outcome of those decisions was always worth more than the money. When I thought I would not have enough money, He would answer, even if that answer was *No* — like the answer I received once when my patience was thin and I was near the end of my rope concerning our living situation.

I remember the time I pursued a new apartment because I believed I deserved it and needed out of my current situation. I drove over to see the place...and I put a plan in motion to rent it, even though God was not leading me to do that.

I went to work and waited for the yes or no but I still hadn't heard anything by the time I left to meet my husband for lunch. While we were at lunch the phone call came with the owner's answer. Yes. Great!

But the next morning I'd settled the outcome in my mind. I would call my best friend and ask for a loan for the deposit. I was preparing a meal when my phone's message alert sounded. A text from Cheryl's husband, the pastor. I looked at my phone in complete disbelief. Her husband often sent scriptures out, but I knew God had chosen this one especially for me. The message was from Psalm 37:21: *The wicked borrow and never repay, but the godly are generous givers.*

After reading that verse, I knew I could not proceed in this direction — trying to borrow and make my own way out. Instead I would have to wait and trust God's direction.

Humans are as God describes us in the Bible. Just like sheep. You see, sheep need a shepherd because they are the most forgetful animals. They will forget and wander away as quickly as they were guided and directed. Also, they actually learn to recognize their shepherd's voice when they hear it, and to follow only their shepherd. It's quite amazing to think how they are so forgetful yet they can remember one voice out of many.

I love the references to sheep!

It was now approaching the end of September and I was still living in that small two-bedroom one-bath house. In the midst of all the Godly events I was still struggling daily for thankfulness and contentment.

So I drove to the salon one day, begging God for a

time frame. Something. Anything to grasp onto. He whispered clearly, "October." October rolled around and the relative and her husband who had been living with us informed us they were moving into a new apartment unit where she worked. They moved in December, and I thought we would finally have some space. Soon, though, we would come to see that tiny house be similar to the amazing provision of Jesus when He fed the 5,000. (John 6.)

Speaking of provision, during this time, my husband had a job that was completely different from his previous line of work. In this job there were incentives in the form of gift cards. I remember one day of almost letting fear in even though God had previously told me to kill fear. My job had called to tell me I had no clients that day. I had $10. No gas. And I probably needed food for dinner. Soon, my husband texted me the verse Psalm 46:10. I knew the Lord wanted me to Be Still and Trust in Him. Soon after that I went to check the mail and found a $25 Target gift card.

God provided those gift cards all year and into the holidays. I even used them to buy Christmas gifts.

On another note, I felt myself not fitting in to Young Life–Wyldlife, the middle school realm ministry I was involved in. I failed as a leader but grew in the failure. On my drive home one day I felt prompted to go home and pray. After arriving home, I sat on the floor and instead of being quick to pray, I tried opening Instagram. The App was black and — I kid you not — would not open. I tried shutting it off and turning it back on. Still nothing! So I thought, *Okay, God is not kidding.* I shut my eyes and waited on what to pray about. Young Life immediately came to mind.

I confessed how I felt out of place. I said, "Lord you clearly led me to this. What is my purpose in their organization?" Once I finished my prayer, my Instagram App opened with no problem. The first photo to pop up was of a mom and baby. The caption read "Please come serve this summer at a Young Lives camp."

Young Lives?

Researching it, I saw Young Lives was under the banner of Young Life, however, their ministry reached out to teen moms across the globe. And I, having been a teen mom, felt the immediate "YES, this is the one!"

I went running after Jesus and His plan for me in this. I had wanted to go serve as a nanny for them but it was too expensive so I prayed. *God if you want me to nanny you will provide a way.* A few weeks before camp started, I got a call that they needed a nanny. And I was financially covered. They also called back asking if one of my daughters could come as well. Shortly after that, we were driving to Oregon to watch babies.

Even more amazing, today that teen mom is now a Young Lives leader.

One night at camp while walking the baby around before getting some sleep, I ran into Libby, one of the summer staff girls, coming from clubroom where the teen moms were. Tears streamed down her face.

"Are you okay?" I asked.

Libby replied, "I'm great. I was in the club room and I felt a little voice inside telling me to hug this teen mom. I thought that was weird but felt the prompting again. So I walked down and wrapped my arms around this girl. She crumpled in my arms and said, 'I just asked God if He was real to send someone to hug me.'"

CHAPTER 26

DRY WELLS

F ast forward to the next winter. I was slammed, working twelve hours some days, still having stories pour out of me or into my life.

Then everything ground to a halt. My books were empty and I couldn't get any appointments. My work schedule became so dried up I was facing not being able to pay my station rent the next month.

I thought about what Christa had said to me one day, "Natalie sometimes the Lord dries up the well to force you in another direction. That was it. It was happening before my eyes and yep, rent was due and I had no way to pay it. I felt the prompting, *You are done here.*

The day I knew quitting was my only option, fear washed in to try and overwhelm me. You see fear comes only from the enemy. God's Word says in 1 John 4:18, *Such love has no fear, because perfect love expels all fear. If we are afraid, it is for fear of punishment, and this shows that we have not fully experienced his perfect love.*

I remember arriving at home after work and entering my bedroom where I found my middle daughter. I was so overwhelmed I said, "I hate this. I hate this house. I hate this life."

She looked at me and said, "What? That is ridiculous!" Then she laughed.

When she left the room, I went into fight mode. Picking up my Bible I opened it. And out loud I declared, "Devil, leave!" I continued, "When this book is open you cannot speak to me or stand. Amen!" The fear left and my mind was cleared to pray and hear God's leading.

Vicki also has a story about spiritual warfare.

There came a time when everything in my life seemed to be like a boat being tossed by waves and flipped bottom side up. I bought Chip Ingram's book *The Invisible War — What Every Believer needs to Know about SATAN, DEMONS, AND SPIRITUAL WARFARE*, and read it cover to cover. Ingram wrote that the devil is created, therefore not omniscient or infinite. He can be resisted by the Christian: *Humble yourselves before God. Resist the devil, and he will flee from you.*"(James 4:7) And God places limitations on him: *"All right, you may test him,"* the Lord said to Satan. *"Do whatever you want with everything he possesses, but don't harm him physically."* (Job 1:12)

After reading Ingram's book, I spoke with a friend who had been in ministry in Guatemala and Peru. He loaned me eight books on spiritual warfare. I soon learned that Satan wasn't afraid of me when I'd been sitting in the pew content to listen to sermons, had beaten the crowd to my favorite restaurant, then gone home to enjoy the rest of my day. But when I got out of the pew and got busy with God's work, he and his creepy friends took notice. Spiritual warfare began when I took a dive into ministry work. That's when I began to get that strange feeling — what I was to later find out was oppression from the spirit world. They didn't like me writing about Jesus. Or teaching about God and His Holy Spirit.

Could demons be real? I'd always believed it but to personally experience something from the dark side — no thanks.

The more I studied the Bible, I had to reconcile myself to the fact that if Jesus is alive and well today, so are demons. And the devil is still roaming the earth trying to find someone to devour.

The friend who'd been in ministry in Guatemala began to tell me stories that happened to him while he served there...stories shocking enough to "curl my hair."

Another woman I spoke with had volunteered to serve in Africa. I asked her about demon possession there — if she'd ever experienced anyone having this problem on "the dark continent." She replied, "Oh, yes. There's a lot of idol worship there and many people worship animals. One man was exorcised of his demons but one culprit apparently didn't want to leave. The man had become a Christian, however, every time he stepped into our church, he began to bray uncontrollably like a donkey when he heard the name of Jesus."

And there were a couple of stories from friends about playing around with the Ouija board — stories that made me never want to touch one.

Possession is easy. Exorcism for some, apparently is not — according to the braying donkey fellow's experience — though many think a Christian cannot be possessed. (I'm no authority on the subject and perhaps God will answer that question once we are with Him in heaven.)

So like my friend who'd one day "cleaned house" by praying over each window, door, and room, I did the same. And I felt like a weight had been lifted.

CHAPTER 27

DIGGING UP WEEDS

Some months before my "Devil, leave!" episode, a friend told me about a nanny website. I was curious. As I sat on my bed, I felt prompted to go to that site and apply. *I mean, I love kids, but nanny? Really?*

I was also looking at an app for a certain picture to post. The photo was of a girl holding balloons jumping or leaping into faith — or rather this photo helped bring to print her "leap of faith." I had saved it and now couldn't find it.

I came across another photo with a girl with a caption, "God is within her, she will not fail." I said, "Yes, let's post this one," not even realizing I was opening my Bible to read from the text that had been paraphrased or condensed to this one short thought. I suddenly realized that the idea for the caption was taken from Psalm 46, a psalm written during turmoil. And the meaning of "Be still and know..." is to know that God is the conqueror so, be still. Let Him do his work.

The original Hebrew words in this verse could be translated: *"Cease striving and know that I am God...."* He was speaking clearly: Trust this path.

I applied for the nanny job.

About an hour after I applied, a woman named Carla contacted me: "I believe you are the answer to our prayers." WOW!

So, soon there I was in a coffee shop interviewing for a whole new role...nanny to three kiddos. At the interview the pay structure was discussed and I was so thankful thinking, *Yes, Lord you are going to finally bless me financially.* (Ummmm, hello-o-o, I am blessed always; but I always want more).

The first day of my new job, I arrived just as Carla was heading out. Her phone rang. And right in front of my eyes and ears, before I even had a chance to begin my new job, I witnessed a conversation about her husband just losing his job. I tried my best to encourage her with my very own testimonies of experiencing the same situation. I said, "You must lean in and onto Jesus. He is the way and strength through this trial."

I later received a text asking me to still take the job but also telling me there would be a huge pay decrease. I felt the Lord saying go and do it. Oh boy! Did I ever struggle in months to come, sitting in a house with three littles feeling as if my gift was being stifled. I felt as if my purpose in life was dying and I struggled with barely making enough money to buy the gas to drive back and forth. I stayed because on days when I really wanted to quit, God sent a verse like Philippians 2:3. *Don't be selfish; don't try to impress others. Be humble, thinking of others as better than yourselves.*

In other words, don't do anything out of selfish ambition. Hold others higher than yourself always looking to serve. It can be a hard lesson to learn.

One day I cried out to God. "Please send me two words. Either 'Be still' or 'Move on.'" I was hoping for a clear road ahead; I wanted to so desperately move on. Once again God used my husband in a way I'd never thought would happen. He sent me a text: "Be Still." I thought, *Oh no! Really? Ewwwww. Not what I was looking for.*

That following Monday I woke with a heavy heart. I didn't want to go babysit; I figured the dad was probably off and home. Soon, Carla messaged. Her husband was at home…for the entire week, and the next week, she would be off from work as well.

You might say I got what I asked for…and also no money. Double edged sword, right? As I sat at home that day, I began to hear the Holy Spirit whisper to me. "Natalie where is your heart? Is it set on me, Jesus?

"Do you nanny for money or to serve?" Sadly, my answer was money. Then He dug deeper. "Do you want to speak to show off your faith or to show Me?" Jesus can dig deep down can't He? Into those places no one sees or reveals. He can show people their true interior motives while on the outside they may profess something else. Do I do what I do to further the kingdom, or is there a small, deep space where I do it for my own motives?

That day, I laid the burden of money at the feet of Jesus. I honestly wanted nothing more than to serve and be made into the image of Jesus. (An image that will never be fully perfected until He returns.)

In this experience was such compassion, love, and mercy. God revealed the ugliness and true heart in this matter, not to condemn me but to dig up those weeds and plant a new, true faith. Faith that says, "Money or no money, I will serve the Lord."

No doubt I was being corrected, for it is by His Fatherly love that correction comes.

CHAPTER 28

GROWING UNSHAKEABLE FAITH

The next Wednesday, I had planned to hike and go out to breakfast with ladies from Bible study. I had very little money as usual, and breakfast would be too much so I chose to drive home instead of going with them. At home I began reading where I'd left off in the Old Testament, the book of 2 Samuel. I had often struggled with the Old Testament and I wanted to finish what I'd started.

But that day I remembered a book Christa had suggested I read in 2010, a book titled *In a Pit with a Lion on a Snowy Day*.

I discovered the book was crafted from the story found in 2 Samuel 23:20: *There was also Benaiah son of Jehoiada, a valiant warrior from Kabzeel. He did many heroic deeds, which included killing two champions of Moab. Another time, on a snowy day, he chased a lion down into a pit and killed it.* Well, now I was intrigued. I knew I had to read it, so I immediately bought the ebook. And I do not exaggerate, I flew through the pages, pumped, because my life was in that book.

I realized that all of the events I'd gone through were lining up not to stress me out or punish me. They were designed to grow me; to grow a little spark of faith into unshakeable Faith. God was testing me in the fire — refining me like silver and purifying me as gold

I once heard this amazing little tale. A silversmith puts the silver in the fire and then when he takes it out, it shines a little, then he puts it back in the fire and keeps at this process until he can see his reflection in the piece after all of the dross is gone and the silver is refined. This process is similar to God's way of perfecting His children.

The word Sovereign is often used to describe God. By definition the word means a supreme ruler, absolute, unrestricted, boundless, ultimate, total, unconditional, ruling, royal, Sovereign Control.

Look at that beautiful list, God in ALL HIS GLORY.

By July 2017 as I was writing I was also taking time to go through my old journals. I sit in awe, because looking back I see that God has, indeed, shown me His great Sovereignty. He truly is in full control. As I see through my journals how the plan for me has unfolded, I see my life's journey in a different light.

I now understand that some people go to church and are consumers. They consume, but never change or "do." Some attend church and grow and learn and allow God to mold them. They truly want to be the clay and let Him be the potter. I'm one of the latter. I'm not making that statement from arrogance, but with humility. I've known from the time I was a small child that I had some sort of inner reverence for God. As a young woman, I grew to realize I am nothing more than a speck of sand in the big scale of things on earth, and from there, the galaxy.

Yet this little speck of sand God made has a heart and a soul. From outside the Milky Way and beyond what Hubble can see the Sovereign God is watching His creation. He wants to be in a relationship with His children. In His Word He's always saying, "Return to me." Because of His longing to have us, His creation, return to Him because He loves us so much, I want to know and grow and be consumed with what He has to say and Who He is.

I guess that makes me a bit of a stalker. I often joke that I have all of these amazing events happen because I stalk God all day.

But back to the nanny life and how that episode turned out — and what being still for that moment was looking like for me.

That stretch of my life was quite a struggle. I felt I was drowning there. And outside of the job, I could not get the Young Lives ministry up and running in my town. I prayed. Reached out. Nothing. Then one day, I was driving to the house where I "nannied," and I cried out to God again. *Why God? Why do you have me here?* Once again, that voice I'd come to know in the depths of my soul answered. *I have brought you to these moments because one day, you will be in front of teen moms and you will get to tell them that no matter what, they just need me (Jesus).* I cried even harder and in full surrender said, "Okay. I'm in."

Months after I submitted in that area, God opened a door from out of nowhere. It was a Friday in August, and I was in a store with the kids when my phone rang. On the other end was a woman asking me if I could come by her salon that evening for an interview. I thought this was crazy. I wasn't looking to do nails again. That night I prayed.

Eventually I ended up in front of a beautiful old home. As I entered I thought *This is the salon of my dreams.* Not only was it beautiful, the main wall had a Bible verse painted on it. I sat with the owner and manager, sisters who were also Christians, and I felt like *Wow! God, here we go.* I came home that night and showed my husband the place online and explained everything that had previously happened. He seemed okay with the idea of me working there.

I left to quickly pick up our daughter. When I returned, I was in for quite a shock. The situation I walked into was like the devil had come in and taken up residence on my couch. My husband was up in arms, "But you never made a lot of money in that industry!"

Surprisingly enough, I stayed calm. And because

of my calm, I knew that my growth and maturity in knowing God was evident. Instead of retaliating with the usual hard words, I removed myself to the bathroom and from any argument. There, I prayed. *God, you see what's happening. Please help.* Finally, I went into my room and heard in my spirit the words from Colossians 3. These were verses about the new person believers can become in Christ. The message also talked about a Christian home life and what that looks like.

That night, I prayed for a dream and God sent me one. In the dream, my husband and I were fighting over money. We then entered an elevator that flipped upside down and became stuck. In the dream I remembered thinking, *We are running out of air. I should tell these other people about Jesus.* Then I woke up and as soon as I was lucid, deep down in my soul I heard, *The wages of sin is death.* (Romans 6:23) You see, the sin was the arguing and bitterness and everything else that goes with all of that and the totality equaled death in a relationship. Instead of arguing, it was best for me to extend forgiveness and pray.

Funny thing: After I was awake I couldn't sleep. Turning on the television, I landed on a story about Ruth. Go figure. At this point in my life I supposed I always felt like God and His Word were my God given passion and purpose. The money didn't faze me.

After a few more discussions with my husband and

understanding — finally — on his part, I was on my way to begin a new journey. When God gave me the new job He also gave me this verse in Revelation 3:8: *"I know all the things you do, and I have opened a door for you that no one can close...."*

The next Thursday morning, May 8, I was sitting in the car in a parking lot working on a Bible study before I had to arrive at the salon. I heard that other annoying voice — the one that always whispered negativity and lies. You see, I wouldn't receive a paycheck for two weeks and had $7 in the bank. I also had a God-ordained dinner coming up that Monday and my gas tank was already on "E." Instead of giving into fear I said, "Stop talking to me!" Then I called out to my Savior, "Lord what do *You* say about all this?"

I heard, "Go to the salon." Obeying, I drove across town with my gas gauge registering on "E," figuring a client or two would tip in cash that day. In the middle of the day, Anna, a close friend from Bible study, messaged me that God told her to provide the food for my dinner on Monday. I replied, "A simple Target gift card would be great!" At the end of the day with my last client in the seat, in walked Anna. She said, "I went to get you a gift card but the Lord told me to give you this instead." And she handed me a one hundred dollar bill. Tears flooded my eyes because the All Knowing sees and knows our every need.

Later, when I slid behind the steering wheel I texted her a picture of my gas gauge. I wrote, "He knew and you didn't." I also prayed the next Saturday morning for provision to celebrate my daughter's birthday the next day. I wondered what surprises were in store.

CHAPTER 29

NICE SURPRISES

F or my daughter's birthday, we usually went to a local beach. This year, we needed a little bit of food and gas to be able to do even that. I had only a handful of clients and no one tipped cash, only credit.

With a few hours of work left, I had an empty schedule. Across from me, a woman — Deborah — was getting her hair colored. I felt prompted to offer her a free manicure, so I introduced myself and she accepted my offer. Like many times in days before, Jesus came into the conversation.

Deborah shared with me how she had seen the salon online and had been drawn to come because of the scripture posted on the website...the same one painted on the wall. She called and asked the receptionist, "Is this a Christian salon?" and was a little taken aback by the woman's response: "I have no idea, let me ask." Not that it mattered if the salon was Christian owned or not, but she said she felt everyone who worked at the salon should have known the answer to that question.

"That response would have normally thrown me off. Still, I proceeded to give the salon a try and now here I am with you, chatting about Him. How wonderful!"

With her services finished, on her way out she turned and walked over and handed me a $50 tip. A few hours later and after I'd cleaned up my station, I got ready to leave and grabbed my purse and phone. There, under my phone, was a $25 gas gift card. There was no one around. No way could I explain this nice surprise.

CHAPTER 30

BLIND FAITH

Even though I had thought my new salon was the salon of my dreams, I soon realized otherwise.

But I also realized I would always feel a spiritual battle no matter where I was. Not between the people, for I loved them all. The battle was between what God had originally established for me and what my focus had become.

I'd always felt the pull. Now I struggled to build or even maintain a clientele. I couldn't understand why God had brought me to that location because it seemed I made less money there than any other place I had worked. I constantly wanted to quit. Each time, He nudged me with a "Not yet." So I stayed.

I soon began having deep and amazing conversations with the younger sister, who styled my hair. Those conversations stirred fire in our souls. One day, God gave me the idea to do nails with no set price on Saturdays. Instead, I could hand over a card with info on Young Lives and they could donate any amount. The results from this plan proved to be a great way for some of the girls to see Him work. The first Saturday, a woman gave $80, another gave $40, etc.

I didn't have too many godly things going on in this particular salon, or perhaps that's only how I perceived things, but I do recall one encounter, with Evie. She and her husband were having an exceptionally hard time conceiving a child. Evie told me how they had visited a relative's church and walked to the front for prayer. The pastor prayed for her and then he told her to go tell everyone she would soon be pregnant. I asked, "Did you do that?"

"No," she replied. "I shared this experience with a family member who told me people would think I was crazy and not to repeat what the pastor told me to anyone."

I felt the Holy Spirit stir within me and I relayed, "We have to step out in faith in order to receive what God has for us. If we don't step out, we stay back and miss out. We must have blind faith."

CHAPTER 31

REQUIRED TO BE FAITHFUL

Eventually, my job began to dwindle to nothing, and once again I wanted to quit. We had scheduled monthly meetings with a woman who ran a program we used in the salon to gain and keep clients.

I didn't think the methods were for me; the "conversation starters" we were encouraged to use with clients weren't natural. The sole focus of the program seemed to be on money. More and more money.

One night before my meeting, God had me write a timeline of my manicurist career. He also kept giving me a verse…Matthew 6:33: *Seek ye first the Kingdom of God, and his righteousness; and all these things shall be added unto you.*

I called Christa looking for advice on my upcoming meeting. Was I really supposed to march in with this paper in hand detailing my manicurist career and the way I received my clients and explain, "Hey, I can't do this program you're expecting me to adhere to. It's not working for me."

It's hard to tell someone who is running a for-profit

business that you aren't there to make money. It sounds crazy. But here's the thing: Yes, jobs are for making money; but God places us where He needs us to be, and in turn provides for us. Therefore, we don't have to strive. We are required to be faithful and He will send the rain on the seed and produce the harvest.

Christa never answered her phone and I didn't get an answer to my burning question so the following morning, as I was driving I asked, "God are you sure about this? As I glanced in the rear view mirror I saw a huge rainbow. No doubt He was reminding me, always, of His promises.

About thirty minutes before my meeting Christa returned my call and I quickly explained the scenario to her. She responded with *"Seek ye first the kingdom of God...."* I cried. And knew this message was from God. Walking into the salon, I felt that lying voice again whispering, "If you read that paper you'll be fired." I mean, really! Why did I care? I'd tried to quit several times already. Right? Then I heard God say, "Remember that verse I gave you?"

You see, when God initially gave me the job, He gave me a verse from the book of Revelation. Verse 3:8: *"I know thy works: behold, I have set before thee an open door, and no man can shut it: for thou hast a little strength, and hast kept my word, and hast not denied my name."* (KJV)

I entered the salon and the meeting. The woman I was to hear speak began her message. When she finished, the

Lord let me have the floor and with boldness I shared about His work in my life. I began with when I started in this industry without Him and then progressed into how I allowed Him to start directing my walk down my paths. The response I received was wonderful and positive and included, "Okay. You don't have to use this system."

Woo-hoo!

But alas, still no growth.

One day, while hanging in the back of the salon with the manager, I vented about how I couldn't understand the lack of nail clients. She said, "May I offer some advice?"

"Of course," I said.

She then said, "I know as Christians we are to share the Gospel and Jesus, but maybe you talk about Him too much." Outraged by her words, I wanted to quit that second but the Spirit of God said, "Not yet."

That night, I was up late wrestling with what my manager had said. *Did I blabber on? Did I talk about Jesus too much? Was she right and was I imagining all of these things?* Oh my.

It was late and I figured my best friend, Ansley, would be asleep. Overcome with doubt about all of this...and my faith...I texted her anyway and vented about how I was so saddened by the words. "Was my faith and all imaginary?" My phone trilled and I couldn't believe this woman of great discernment was awake. She said these awesome words — are you ready? "Hey baby girl!

I've had a few margaritas but the Holy Spirit can cut through anything!" That response had me laughing and crying at the same time. She then quoted from the book of Revelation. "Nat, the angels in heaven sing Holy, Holy, Holy, is the Lord God Almighty day and night without ceasing. You could never talk about Him too much." She wasn't kidding!

That was the Holy Spirit. And her reply was all I needed to remind me of the truth. I was still having incredible faith-filled conversations with clients here and there. I realized I was actually at the salon for a way bigger purpose.

On one Wednesday night I dropped off one of my daughters at church so she could attend her youth group meeting. Dressed so bummy, I dragged myself into our church's coffee shop anyway. A friend asked me to join her in the chapel. It was the first night of a new women's Bible study.

As I sat in that study I heard clear as day why I was placed in the salon for work and specifically, the person I was to reach. Someone at the salon had wandered off from her race with Jesus and He asked me to go pick her back up.

He is so wonderful! And He will rearrange other people's lives, schedules, etc., if they're willing and available. He positions us in the right place to bring others to Himself and for His ultimate glory.

God loved this woman so much that he sent me to her…and wouldn't let me quit until He made it clear *He* was what she needed. He had never left and He was adamant He was to be first in her life.

Soon after all was made right, God gave me the okay to leave. The battle was never with the women of the salon. I loved them all. The battle was not of flesh and blood, the battle was of a spiritual nature. Pretty astonishing how in that Bible study, with me in my bummy clothes and all, a message rang out loud and clear. Our "place" contains the plan of God. Where we are is where we have a purpose.

I recently heard an astounding quote by Jill Briscoe: "Go where you're sent. Stay where you're put, unpack and give what you've got until you're done." That seems to be my motto these days. Truly, I believe it is because I have previously prayed some reckless prayers. Wiser in my walk now, I have now realized I simply need to answer God with the words I've said a ton of times, "Lord, send me. Here I am."

CHAPTER 32

A Few Moments for Eternal Impacts

After that salon, my nail chapter closed for a bit. Adventures anew awaited elsewhere that would challenge and continue to grow me and my faith. The previous summer after a successful Young Lives camp, I had an opportunity to attend a Young Lives summit for training in Oregon.

The trip started off with changed plans. No surprise; that's often the case. I was supposed to fly out with another woman — a woman who, to me, was more qualified for the main coordinator role. After she cancelled, I found myself alone at the airport for an early flight. As I stood in line, the man in front of me read my sweatshirt. "Are you going on vacation?" he asked.

"No," I replied. "I'm off for a training weekend for a teen mom ministry." He gave me a quizzical look and an "Okay" and turned back to his wife and kids. Something was drawing his attention to what I'd said, though, and spurred him on to converse with me. He spun around and asked, "What you said, what does that mean?"

I began to share with this man — Charles — how

Jesus had called me to follow Him into the lives of teen moms and build relationships with them so in turn they earned the right to be heard. The right to share the Gospel of Jesus. Charles then said, "That seems good."

He then shared some of his faith with me, and as we finished our conversation I said, "I'll see you in heaven." Charles freaked out. "You can't say that. You can't be telling me that. You don't know for sure you're going to heaven."

"Yes. I do," I said. He began to explain to me how his Catholic background and faith says you never know for sure if you're going to heaven, and maybe if you enter this middle ground you can work your way to heaven.

Hmmmmmm. This belief goes against the very point of Ephesians 2:8-9, that tells us: *God saved you by his grace when you believed. And you can't take credit for this; it is a gift from God. Salvation is not a reward for the good things we have done, so none of us can boast about it.*

Charles and I parted ways once through the security checkpoint. As I walked in the other direction he ran over to me and asked, "Can I email you some of my writings about my time with God?"

"Of course. I'd love that," I replied.

He handed me his business card and I gave him my email address. Within a few hours he emailed me about a wonderful experience of taking communion. What he wrote was beautiful to read.

A week later, before Bible study, I emailed Charles and explained how he could be sure of his salvation by using Scripture. God had given me many references to share with him. Then while at Bible study the speaker mentioned a verse in Ephesians as well. It was a verse about the armor of God. One of the verses she quoted was Ephesians 6, which is about the Helmet of Salvation. She said we must put the helmet on, an analogy symbolizing a helmet or covering that protects our minds...all pointing to the Bible's teaching that we are saved in Jesus. I explained all of this in my email to the new friend I'd met at the airport.

The next morning Charles responded to my email, not with a concrete "Yes" or with an "Okay, I agree," but with proof of how God speaks to us. Here was his proof: He told me that the previous Sunday while at mass, the priest spoke on that very same verse! I was stunned as always about how God brings people together to speak through messages and conversations. Charles and I stayed connected for awhile but then lost touch.

The crazy thing about the people who come in and out of our lives is that we sometimes may never see them again. We have those few moments to make eternal impacts, and then poof! They're gone.

CHAPTER 33

Do Not Put God
in a Box

After the summit it was back to building Young Lives. We had two teen moms and an outreach to grow and be faithful with even if we were given just one teen. After meeting with my area director I was offered a part time staff position with a little pay if I could raise the money. This was my big opportunity to show what God had taught me about His character as the provider of all things.

The area director explained how it would be great to start with a $5,000 donation. I left the meeting and typed up my donor letter. When I had the area director edit the letter before I sent it out, she mentioned that I had not put a dollar amount in it. I explained, "I don't want to put God in a box. What if He wanted to give more or less? God already knows what I need and what girls will be involved. He already knows the details."

I mailed out only a handful to start with. In the meantime, I met weekly with the two young women for Bible study. One day, as I was leaving the house there I received a phone call from a woman named Jennifer at my church. The congregation is fairly large so I didn't know who Jennifer was. I pulled my car over to chat with her. She let me know she had heard that I was mentoring teen moms. "How's the ministry going?"

I explained the heart of Young Lives and how God led me to the organization. Jennifer then shared how the church had financially assisted a teen mom and paid for her to attend college. She'd graduated a semester early. Then Jennifer said, "We'd like to donate to you. Do you have a dollar amount?" I was silent for a bit. "I wasn't ignoring you," I said. "I was waiting on God to give me the answer. I put all of my trust in him so whatever you would like to give will be enough because He already knows our need."

Jennifer then said, "The amount we'd like to give is $5,000."

Yes! Praise you Jesus! He nailed it once again!

CHAPTER 34

SIT BACK AND LET GOD

F or some time my sole focus was on Young Lives. In that same year, one of my Young Lives girls, Susan, needed a place to live and God had prompted my family to move her in with us. I was a bit nervous about her coming to live with my family because we still lived in a two-bedroom house. Even so, the move began.

To make matters more "up close and personal," my young adult cousin had moved in after my eldest child had moved to college. And now this young mom and her one-year-old daughter were joining us…but believe it or not, we had two empty closets. Yes, unbelievable!

Susan and her baby girl slept in one bed. My seventeen-year-old slept with the twenty-five-year-old cousin, and my youngest teen claimed the sofa.

Yes, this is a real story. The camaraderie was so beautiful and so difficult. All girls. And surprisingly enough, not once did anyone fight over the bathroom. That had to be God!

This all took place around December 2015. The crazy thing was, the owner of our rental had listed the house for sale. So with all of us squeezed in, we also had to clean and make the house presentable for showings.

The house sold in that same month and the new owners graciously extended the offer to continue renting. We had no intentions of moving, however, the buyers backed out of the purchase. January arrived and new buyers were in the picture. They, too, extended an offer to stay, and again, we were content to stay put. However, this sale also fell through. Okay. "Third time's a charm" they say, so there it was: New buyers. And this time we had to be out by February 28th.

Now we really needed God to move in a mighty way. I went online searching for a new rental home, I felt the Holy Spirit prompting and telling me I would not find our next place online. I would have to wait for God to direct my steps. To be honest, that scenario was scary and I failed quite a few times.

But one Wednesday, I drove Susan to get her hair done. I was overwhelmed that day. Such a struggle. Where was everyone to go? Where was *I* to live? While Susan was at her appointment, I sat in the car with the sleeping baby and there I was saying, "God what do I do? I can quote a ton of scriptures but none are helping. Please, please talk to me today. I know you are with us but please just speak to me like you have before. Please send me something!"

I was clinging to hope by the tips of my fingers and trying to not let doubt and worry creep in. The hair appointment taken care of, there was time to spare before picking up my daughter from work. I ran to the bookstore to grab a book I'd been wanting to read. I stepped over to another aisle to check out the Bibles there. In the middle of the aisle, however, sat a man who had pulled up a chair and placed himself rather righteously in front of the Bibles.

This is so odd. Who puts a chair in the aisle in front of books and Bibles?

He looked over at me and asked, "What are you looking for?"

I replied, "A journaling Bible. One that has margins you can write in." He reached over and pulled a Bible out, but it wasn't what I had in mind. He then asked, "Do you want to know what my gift from God is?"

"Sure," I answered. What else did I have to lose that day other than time?

He then began to tell me how God prompted him to read scripture to youths. How he had gone up to this fifteen-year-old and read him what God told him to read. The young man had broken down in tears because the scripture perfectly fit the situation he was going through.

Then the man said, "I'll read you one." *Are you kidding me? No way is this happening.* He reached forward, grabbed a Bible off the shelf, and flipped the pages to the very chapter I love. Psalm 46. This psalm was written during battle and in that psalm is a special verse. *Be still and know I AM GOD....* (v. 10)

God nailed it through the Bible aisle man!

God was once again reminding me to, "Be still and know." He knew exactly where I would live and how. "Be still" — because He was going to reveal to me where I would live and He would make it happen.

I looked at this man and with joy exclaimed, "Do you know the kind of day I am having? I had literally cried out to God for a word because I'm afraid of becoming homeless in a few weeks. And now this!"

He then asked, "Do you know Ephesians 6?"

"Yes. The chapter is about putting on the whole armor of God."

"Well, put it on. You know you're not fighting against anything other than evil." He mentioned some other things and then prayed over me right there in the aisle. The entire event was mind bending.

Yet when the following Saturday arrived, I still failed to believe. I found myself consumed with fear since nothing was happening, and where we lived the cost of living was astronomical.

So there I was, home all alone, as I found myself once again scrolling through the internet. I'd begun to look in less expensive neighborhoods that were near our present house. I found a nice home that would increase our commutes and pull us away from a lot of current activities but maybe, just maybe, this house was the one for us.

I called and spoke with the woman who needed to rent it out as soon as possible. She was willing to meet me at the house that afternoon and if I could bring the deposit, the house would most likely be ours. I didn't have the deposit, but I was blessed to have had a woman come into my life who would be willing to give me such a gift. I quickly humbled myself and asked her by text for a loan. She responded immediately with, "Yes, no problem."

Suddenly, it seemed as though a wave washed over me with a reminder of the verse about how it was wicked to borrow. I believed God was saying, "*Do not do this.*" I sat there, frozen. What had I done? Instead of trusting God completely, I had cried many tears as fear flooded through me.

Now I cried out to God with my fear. Then I sent my friend a message and said I could not take the money. She replied, "No. You can take the money. It's not a loan, I am giving it to you." I felt this uncertainty in my heart, but thought I would drive over to her house. Then right before I was heading out, my text message alert sounded.

My husband had copied a text from a relative of his and sent it to me: "I have been feeling like I should text this, and today, especially. There is a large three bedroom apartment available where I work. We can all move in together and save money."

To be honest my heart sank because I knew this was from God and this was His answer. At the same time I was upset because I longed for my own space and this seemed like another trial to overcome.

You see, this relative and I were very different. And living with people is not easy. There is my human side, which always fails miserably at extending grace often, or extending mercy, compassion, or sincere love. Then there's the "not judging others" thing….

My list goes on and on.

But this is why the Gospel is so powerful in my life. Without the strength of Jesus in me these things are simply impossible. But God often nudges me, corrects me, convicts me, and grows me in these areas. Yet, oftentimes I still fail. I've learned that 2 Timothy 2:13 true. *If we are unfaithful, he remains faithful, for he cannot deny who he is.*

So there we were, moving out to a new area and a new place that was no doubt ordained by God. As I moved to this new area of town, summer was fast approaching, and with it, Young Lives camp. I questioned attending camp because Young Lives just wasn't growing in the city where I'd started it.

Sometimes it is easy to strive to do something rather than completely sit back and let God do His work. I have learned one jaw-dropping thing about God's character: If the work is of Him it will happen. There will be results. There is no need for striving or perfection. What's required is simply obedience and trust.

In the end, I decided to go to camp. But there I was heading out with just one teen mom. Even then I considered backing out because this was her third time attending. But God made it clear I was to go, so I did.

Not long after I'd moved, I met a few ladies from an area near where I had moved. Right away I felt a connection with this group of girls and we all hung out during our week at camp.

And did we ever have an awe-inspiring time!

Soon after camp was over God made it clear that my work in the previous area was finished. I reached out a week or so later to the leader of the area nearer where I now lived. We knew each other from previous camp and leader meetings. I explained how her girls had been in contact with me after camp and how I would love to become a volunteer leader for her. I then spoke with our other director, sharing my heart for these ladies and leading in my new area. Neither of them responded to me for a couple of days and I was saddened. I told my husband, "God could be closing the door and this just breaks my heart." Then I prayed and waited.

CHAPTER 35

WINDOWS OF TIME

Soon I was super excited that God still wanted to use me in the ministry. I received an invitation from my new leader to attend an upcoming meeting. So there I was. The woman began speaking to her leaders about her time ending with this work because God was calling her to the high school Young Lives group. I thought, *Oh great. Now this group is ending. How sad!* She added, "I've been praying for about two years now that God would lead someone else to take over here. And I'd like to introduce Natalie. I believe she's the leader God has put in my place." I was brought to tears to think this was God's bigger plan. I was so excited! Then of course I had to laugh. "Hey! So you prayed me over here!"

All of that worrying for nothing. God had a much bigger plan for me all along. I now understood why God had moved me to the new area. There I was, sent just like all the times before.

If you are reading this and are a Christian I want to encourage you. This following-Jesus life is not easy. As a matter of fact I run into doubt and questioning all the time. I sometimes wonder, *Am I crazy? Am I imagining all of this?*

When God is the One opening doors I would never have imagined I could have opened myself, then God is the One arranging my game board.

But this life is no game.

His plans for us come with purpose and are very real. And His word is a great promise. *"If you look for me wholeheartedly, you will find me."* (Jeremiah 29:13)

This Christian walk requires seeking, and time alone with, God. One of my favorite quotes is by a speaker/writer by the name of Jennie Allen. She said, "The only way to do the things God has called us to do, the only way to keep doing it, is with joy, pure hearts and compassion. We must build and sustain a private world. A private world is the space 'you create' only for you and God. It's the truth. You cannot follow Jesus and not be with Jesus."

So I suddenly comprehended I was onto a new adventure with new faces, cities, joys, and heartbreak. All worth it.

As I began to connect the dots with such ease in my new location, I really started to miss doing nails. I started to pray with specific details for a new job. I soon found one and secured an interview. All of the things I prayed for relating to this new job were there, and I was hired. Now things were floating along smoothly: Young Lives and a nail salon with a great atmosphere and lovely coworkers.

Some great surprises were in store for me at this new salon. I found myself sharing the provision part of my testimony quite often. Specifically in the beginning, and with one woman, Donna, in particular. One day she was complaining that the tips from the customers were "no good." (Her exact words.)

"What do you mean?" I asked. "I've come a long way in my life's journey. Money is not what matters to me."

She shrugged, then let out a big sigh. "Money matters to everyone."

"Not to me," I said, "because Jesus has taught me to trust Him as my provider."

She rolled her eyes and went about the day.

That same conversation happened a few more times until one day I had the opportunity to share in more detail. She said, "You're just lucky!"

I replied, "No way it's luck. If I didn't pray or trust in His name alone, I wouldn't have these testimonies to share." One day, I was prompted to buy Donna *Jesus Calling*, the notable devotional book I kept giving away that kept coming back by different means so I could give it away again. I prayed on my way into the salon that morning. "Lord, if you're truly telling me to give this book to her I will see her before going inside." That was to be my sign my gift would be from God.

I parked in my usual spot, the spot where I'd never seen Donna and you guessed it, I saw her that morning.

In fact, I'd never seen her in the parking lot before work until that morning. Yep. There she was parked right across from me and sitting in her car.

I opened her car door, climbed in, and explained the Gospel. I shared the fact that I'm a broken sinner and God loved me so much He sent His son to pay the price for not only my sin, but the sin of ALL. That whoever puts their life and faith in Him receives eternal life and peace and guidance and so much more in this life now. Then I said, "Now that I've been able to explain the Gospel to you, I'd like to give you a little devotional book."

A few weeks later, Donna left the salon. But I knew God's perfect plan had been to have her there for a window of time so I could share with her about His love and provision. Our paths had crossed for that one perfect moment.

CHAPTER 36

RIGHT WHERE YOU ARE

On this journey it has been wonderful to have opportunities to share sermons and even some of the not-so-talked-about parts of faith. Like how the enemy truly comes after us and what his tactics are. Hmmmmm. Maybe that should be my next book. I would love to teach on that subject someday. Only God knows what's in store.

After all of these stories, I can't leave out my hard working manager, Sue, who really went above and beyond her job as a manager.

Sue was a remarkable and awe-inspiring worker who kept growing her skills as a cosmetologist while wearing multiple hats at the salon. She has to be one of my favorite "Godcidents" to write about.

From time to time since the day I had been hired I had been afforded the opportunity of mentioning my relationship with Jesus. Sue responded in kind but she never went too deep.

One day, there was a family emergency with her grandfather. He got back on his feet for a short while and I was afforded the opportunity to meet him, but soon, the part of life we all would rather do without, happened. Sue's grandfather had been a strong man of faith so that was comforting.

Before long, Sue was drawn to the same church where her grandfather had been a member. She then picked up the Bible and began the phenomenal journey of getting to know Jesus and the Word.

I said to her, "Seeing your journey unfold brings me such hope. I can only imagine how much your grandfather prayed for you when he was alive. We never know when or how our prayers might be answered. Even though your grandfather isn't here to see your newfound relationship with Jesus, your grandma is. And one day she'll see your grandfather again and hopefully he'll know the prayers he prayed so well for you came to be." (Today, I still can't wait to see what God has in store for Sue.)

The salon I was in had been such a peaceful part of my journey. I had many hope-filled conversations with clients and coworkers. One day when I was down and feeling distant from Jesus, I began the day by praying for just a little something — anything to remind me He is always with me. That morning, a woman walked into the salon as I was finishing up a pedi. I heard my boss tell her to return in a few minutes when I would be available. I wondered why she hadn't asked my coworker in the back to take her. *Maybe there wasn't enough time,* I thought. Anyway, she did return. She was a bit older than I was and had such style. I complimented her on her great style and said, "I love your short hair."

"Thank you," she replied, "I've been a hairdresser for many years but I recently retired." Later in conversation, she said, "I've had a lot of shoulder pain and have been seeing an excellent local chiropractor." Then out of nowhere came the revelation that she was a Christian. My gaze met hers and I smiled before responding. "I prayed for Him to make His presence known today and He sent you." She replied, "Yes. He did."

And you know, I never saw that woman again!

There *is* that verse from Hebrews 13:2: *Don't forget to show hospitality to strangers, for some who have done this have entertained angels without realizing it!*

God is perfect in his timing, precise in every detail so we full well know certain Godcidents are from Him. He nailed it when it came to the desire of my heart that day. Who can say if she was sent from above?

I'd like to say that if you don't know Him, you should take a moment and think of the many ways He has presented Himself. At sunrise — a new day of life. At sunset — peacefulness almost tangible enough to touch. People — even some you may resent because of their devout faith. Life situations and scrapes you shouldn't have survived — that's mercy. The list goes on.

God is always inviting His children, and will keep inviting and wooing. His desire is to have a relationship with those He created…an eternal relationship where those who love Him can admire, praise, and worship Him forever, just as the Most High deserves. A relationship that allows believers to drop to bended knees in sorrow due to their reckless behavior. A relationship that is a friendship where those who serve Him can be brutally honest and ask bold questions. A relationship where one can bring it all — all cares and woes — because He can handle it all and He cares.

What kind of king or ruler sets his title aside, steps off his throne and enters into a society not his own? Who lowers himself to the level of a servant just to show us that our way of life on this earth should be serving "the least of these" around us. What ruler shares and opens doors to show unconditional love to each and every one of those he rules over? No other God I know.

Most gods or images of gods habitually beg the minds of men so to speak, to do many works to come into their presence. With many rituals and many sacrifices there's always a wanting. But not with Jesus, who being one with God said in so many words, "I created you. I see you. I want to come to you, and and I want you to come to Me." And I might add, "Right where you are."

CHAPTER 37

THE PERFECT SHEPHERD

I'd like to introduce you to one last friend, Fatima. Her story comes into play in 2016. I had called to make a nail appointment with her. I had started to follow her social media page and her talent amazed me. When I called, she scheduled me two months out. Yikes! But I was willing to wait.

The week of my appointment, God had been placing some young ladies — friends of my daughter, Victoria — on my heart to disciple. I asked if they'd be interested.

They all responded with the same day and time available. And wouldn't you know, it was the day and time of my nail appointment with Fatima. I said, "No way! I've been waiting for this appointment."

The night before my appointment, around 10 P.M., Fatima cancelled because she had been sick for some time. I knew the Lord's plan was taking place. So instead of having my nails done, I had coffee and fellowship with the young ladies.

I shared with them that God really wanted us to meet because I had been anticipating this nail appointment for some time and poof! Cancelled. I knew it would be a while before another appointment, so that same day I reached out to another woman I knew who did beautiful nails. She, too, was usually booked a few weeks out but I gave her a ring anyway. Calling me around noon, she said, "My one o'clock cancelled. Can you come then?"

I considered it a little miracle, said yes, and headed over. When I was there I told her and her previous client all about my canceled appointment and how I had obeyed God and He then blessed me with this appointment. She said, "Yes, no one ever cancels, but my one o'clock had a flat tire." Sad for the person with the flat, but inside I was happy dancing about getting my nails done.

A few months later, I tried to schedule with Fatima again and she squeezed me into a seven A.M. appointment. Crazy, huh? The night before — again around ten P.M. — she had to cancel once more. I could sense something going on out of my control. I kid you not, I texted my other gal next day and she had a one o'clock cancellation. When I got there this time she jokingly said, "Natalie you have something special inside or something's going on. I never have people cancel but when you message me, they cancel." I replied, "Yes, I do have something going on. And His name is Jesus." I was able to share about the Savior that day.

Okay. Three times is the charm they say. A while later, I tried calling Fatima one last time and she scheduled me a week later. Woo-hoo! The day I walked in I introduced myself and told her I did nails as well. She said, "Well, I'm on the verge of leaving this career for a different one."

I couldn't believe it. I said, "Are you sure? You are so talented. Why leave? Jesus must have brought me here right on time."

The reason for my assumption? When I first found Fatima on her social media page, her bio gave her name and under it I read, "Trust in Him Always." When I showed up for my appointment this time, she had deleted that little caption. I mentioned my observations to her and she was surprised I had noticed. I then shared, "It seemed like my whole life waiting for an appointment with you, but really Jesus had set us up at the right time."

So one night later, I visited with Fatima and we were both having a venting session. In the midst of our rant God had me sharing stories…while He was speaking to my heart.

As matter of fact, I was angry and didn't even want to speak anymore. I knew what He was doing and how He was reminding me of what He has done, what He has taught me, and wants me to do this time around: Grow and Trust and Be Still and Let Me Fight for You.

The situation with Fatima had its humorous side too. I was telling her how God so calmly sits me down and has me share and share until I am speaking to *myself*. I am always amazed at what a good counselor I have for free!

Now allow me to back up for a minute. In Isaiah Chapter 9 — Isaiah being a book written by the prophet Isaiah approximately 700 years before Jesus' birth — there were prophecies that were so undeniable. In Chapter 9 verse 6, Isaiah mentioned that one of the characteristics of the Messiah to come is that He would be called, among several names, Wonderful Counselor.

That prophecy came true! When I am in need of counsel, His is so perfect. I just need to Be Still and rest in Him.

Now back to Fatima. Today, she is my amazing friend and manicurist. The Lord has truly blessed me with her along with her generous heart.

While I was with my friend getting my nails done recently — I wish you could have seen them, they were a masterpiece but like all masterpieces they were a long time in the making — I was commenting about how forgetful of people most of us are. I shared that all throughout the Old Testament, the resounding theme is: God created a people. They made false gods to worship and forgot the true God. And out of righteous anger He released deserved judgment, yet out of His love and mercy, He restored and redeemed, bringing the people back to Himself. *Are you kidding me? Who does that but a pulchritudinous God?*

No doubt He is wondrously Magnificent!

Jesus expounded on the subject by giving examples of

God's people as His sheep and Himself as the shepherd. I was sharing about a wonderful book I'd read where the writer met a shepherdess and ended up staying at this stranger's house to witness this lifestyle. In the story she told how she immediately thought of the Bible references. While with the shepherdess, the sheep responded only to their shepherd — as I've mentioned before — and when the baby lamb was released from the mom, the shepherdess lured it in and snatched it close. Once this act was performed, she became the shepherdess to that little lamb so it would know her voice.

In John 10, Jesus explained how He is The Good Shepherd and how His followers are His sheep. He explained how His sheep would know His voice, how the good shepherd lays down His life for his sheep. So many beautiful analogies.

I'm listing a few behavioral characteristics of sheep so readers can better understand why God's people would be referred to as sheep in need of a good shepherd.

Here goes:

Sheep are known to be unintelligent and forgetful. Their herd instinct and flock behavior and how quickly they flee and panic make it hard to herd them. They seek light instead of dark places, and high ground. They like the familiar and resist change and are conservative animals that are instinctively fearful. They are not "sheepish" and are sometimes aggressive, especially the rams. Sheep cannot be made to do something contrary to their nature, however, they have a knack for recognizing voices and faces for years. If isolated, they are likely to become stressed.

While researching the habits of sheep, thought by some to be dumb animals, I discovered sheep and humans have some similarities. They don't do well alone, but in a flock they thrive. They are able to stand together and they have a propensity to follow other sheep though they will follow their shepherd, especially accepting his or her presence during the birthing process. Pain quickly changes their minds about needing a shepherd, especially for the females when they are giving birth.

Vicki also has a story to share about sheep.

While in Israel, I noticed the Beduoins out with their sheep on the hillsides. I'd read that even if their flocks were mixed with other shepherds' flocks at a watering place, all a shepherd had to do was call for his sheep and those belonging to him would follow him out, no matter how many flocks were mixed together.

And I once heard a story about how at night, a shepherd would sometimes herd his flock into a fenced in circular area made of stones. The stone fence was no higher than a couple of feet because sheep would never think of jumping out of an enclosed area. They never look up, not even when out grazing on the hillsides. If one jumped over a cliff the others would follow. They wouldn't dare drink water from a moving stream for fear of drowning. With all of that heavy wool, a sheep would sink to the bottom or be swept away in a torrent; somehow they inherently know this. The water has to be "still" water. That's the reason David wrote *He maketh me to lie down in green pastures: He leadeth me beside the still waters...yea, though I walk through the valley of the shadow of death, I will fear no evil; for thou art with me....* (23rd Psalm KJV, the version I memorized as a child.)

The same verse in the NLT reads: *He lets me rest in green meadows; he leads me beside peaceful streams...Even when I walk through the darkest valley, I will not be afraid, for you are close beside me....*

But back to the shepherd who had herded his sheep into a stone pen. After the flock was settled and all were accounted for, the shepherd placed his body within the opening of the pen's door and rested there during the night, becoming the "door" or "gate." And with the shepherd as the door and the sheep's security, the sheep could be counted on to stay in place and rest in safety.

When Jesus told his followers that he was the way, the truth and the life — the door — (John 14:6 and John 10:7) they knew what He meant. He was the only way to heaven. By stating "I am *the* door..." and not "a door," Jesus was declaring that He is the only means by which anyone may receive eternal life (John 3:16)

Note: The NLT reads "gate" instead of "door."

John 10:9 says, *"Yes, I am the gate* (door— KJV). *Those who come in through me will be saved. They will come and go freely and will find good pastures."* The point Jesus was making by saying "I am the gate (door)" is that the Pharisees — enemies of Jesus — were rejecting their only access to God, that access being Jesus. *"Jesus is the one referred to in the Scriptures, where it says, 'The stone that you builders rejected has now become the cornerstone.' There is salvation in no one else! God has given no other name under heaven by which we must be saved."* Acts 4:11-12

I was telling my friend how amazing all of this is: How Jesus desires to shepherd us. To know us. And in turn His children would know His voice, and how we were also created for community and to be together, rarely "flying solo" or staying isolated.

In Genesis 1:26 God says: *"Let us make man in our image."* The Bible says that "in the beginning" God was already a community God, communing with the Son and Holy Spirit. Like sheep in pain, God's people — those who can humble themselves — are especially drawn to a higher power for help.

1 John 5:7 (KJV) tells us: *There are three that bear record* (witness) *in heaven, the Father, the Word, and the Holy Ghost* (Holy Spirit)*: and these three are one.* God created the human species in the image of God; this is why

humans long for community. This is why reaching out and inviting others in is so powerful. Everyone wants to feel wanted — a part of something — and to have purpose. To feel loved. Community is part of the DNA of humans. God designed people with purpose, and in His creation He placed longing for something more along with a feeling for eternity.

Ecclesiastes 3:11 says: *God has made everything beautiful for its own time. He has planted eternity in the human heart, but even so, people cannot see the whole scope of God's work from beginning to end.*

So while I was listing sheep descriptions, tendencies, and characteristics, God was reminding me of what He had taught me.

Right now, I relax with my coffee and a whole new attitude with which I'll respond to those I might meet during my day.

Life is obviously filled with ups and downs. Marriage can seem like one is on a roller coaster at times. But times like these are when I learn to believe in the promises of God. I learn to "Be still" so my God and my Savior can fight for me.

Speaking of fighting for me, remember my mentioning I'd moved to a different town, living with extended family as roommates? An arrangement that is trying to all parties no doubt, especially when having no common ground makes situations more difficult and taxing, to say the least — just like the majority of my life has been.

While living with this extended family, I experienced days of despair. I had an intense longing to be set free. I yearned for my own space and wondered why I was in that particular house for that particular span of time. On many days I felt alone and forgotten and I often cried out in prayer. Others cried out in prayer for me or with me.

I began specifically praying that I would be still and wait on the Lord to move. I prayed that in His time, He would move me to the place He wanted me. I prayed I wouldn't have to go look for that next place, that instead, God would land that sweet spot right in my lap.

That new home was handed right to me. In a new city. And I admit, at first, before I landed the new place, I almost tried to go my own way. I almost wandered away from the shepherd's leading.

A few months earlier, the Lord placed something on my heart. Some people say this feeling or request is like a "burden" to do something that is asked by God. There's an expression, "God has laid a burden on my heart." Well, this burden was real. And the task was difficult. I wanted Him to pick someone else for such a job.

But God cleared the way and opened up the path to complete this job. Finally, I surrendered. There was nothing easy about it, but at last I obeyed. The path was rocky but at last I finished what God had for me to do.

Then God created a circumstance that pushed me and my family right out the door of our home. Again to be uprooted! Searching once more for a place to lay my head, I drove by the address He sent me to. At first sight, I thought, *No, not good enough. I'll find a better place.* Now searching for better, I found mediocre at a higher cost. So I drove back to the first place and thought, *Let me see the inside because the outside looks a bit old.*

Trying to discover if this place would be my new home, as I entered the manager's office I prayed for a direct sign from God. The manager said, "I'd like to rent you a townhouse but I can only show you the inside of an apartment at this time."

"No problem," I said, though disappointed. "I just need a general idea of what the place looks like." The manager then had a change of heart and took me to her personal residence. Wanting me to see the real deal, she allowed me to view her home because it was similar to the unit she had for lease. And there, hanging above her television, was a sign made of iron: "As for me and my house, we will serve the Lord."

Yes! Answered. Done. Nailed it. *"Lord, I. Am. In!"*

And He was faithful in fulfilling my year long prayer. My own space was handed to me and my family along with a peaceful, cute, and huge blessing by way of the wall hanging.

I think my experience searching for a new home

was sort of like church. To some from the outside, the Church looks broken. They see judgmental people, cliques, arrogant people, the rude, the envious, and the self righteous. So looking at this mess, they say, "No thank you, I'll find my own way. I don't want to be with those hypocrites." And they're right: Churches are filled with all those types of people — including me.

I am sorry and must apologize, because we "church people" often get it all wrong. Man gets his hands all over everything and everyone desires to go their own way, do their own thing, creating a church God never intended. But that's because humans are fallible and, being deceived or mistaken, fall short easily. I'll be the first to admit that I, and everyone in those church buildings, need a rescuer.

Some people show up at church to be nothing more than consumers; they can check off the "attended church" box. And then there are some who walk in judging everyone around them. Some come to see and be seen. Some come out of habit. Some come to make business contacts. Some come for information. The list is endless. But God's not interested in any of that because all are broken and in need of a healer. God wants transformation.

Then there are the folks who go to church and grow. Some even recklessly abandon their lives. Some become like one of my favorite verses: *Take delight in the Lord, and he will give you your heart's desires* (Psalms 37:4). When I delight in the Lord, I delight in His character. His heart. His ways. And my desires become His desires.

I see a generation of women who believe God, read His word and want to risk it all — laying it all out there — to show the world this Jesus is real. I know He has changed me and I am far from finished…still a work in progress.

I see others pointing at the manmade church and saying this isn't what God had planned so let's abandon the church and start over. Here's the thing: There is no "perfect church" only a perfect God. So go seek Him. Pray. And when you do He will open a door, because Jesus *is* "the door." Don't expect perfection in people. Only Jesus is perfect. Instead, remember: All are broken and are there seeking Him too.

And in the seeking, you may find what you've always been looking for, if you refrain from judging. Instead of judging the outside, go back and take a closer look inside. If you're attending a Bible centered Gospel church, you can find God.

And what is a Gospel church? *Gospel* means Good News: the good news that while we were yet sinners Christ came and died for us and was resurrected on the third day. The good news that because of His death as the perfect lamb and sacrifice, His followers may die to sin — also crushing sin and death — that those who believe in Christ the Messiah will also live in victory. The good news that the same victory is through Christ.

The good news that whoever believes in Him, the only way to God and salvation will have *eternal* life (hard to believe for some, and not popular these days, but in Acts 4:12 Peter confirmed this by saying there is salvation in no one else besides Jesus). Now that dear friends, is mighty good news. And true.

Now, I've reached the end of some of my most profound Jesus tales from my nail salon chronicles. Thanks for allowing me to share some of my most intimate moments with you. May you be blessed in your walk with the Lord Jesus and know that God has already *nailed it!* for you through the sacrifice of His precious One and Only Son. Allow Him to come into your life to show you how to live your life.

Amen and Amen!

FINAL WORDS

For those reading this book who do know the Savior, I hope these true stories and testimonies bring excitement for more encouragement and trust in Him. I hope that by Vicki and me sharing what God has done for us, more lost souls will surrender through His loving kindness and more of God's people will be able to live in awe of Him and His majestic deeds.

One of my favorite attributes of God is His way of reminding us He is there for His children. On days when I so easily forget all He has done or I second guess whether what I believe is real, or I am so angry and frustrated and can't see an answer or fix to my problem, He reminds me: *I'm here.*

He uses my nail station to do, in general, His will. He has me begin a Godcident story, and while I am sharing He uses my own story to remind me of how He answered my prayers previously. Or, His Holy Spirit brings to mind what He has already taught me. It's expedient that I go back and that I seek His Word and look to what He promises.

Exodus14:14 tells us "stand still for the Lord shall fight for you." (KJV) How many people really stay or stand still or believe before first filling up with anger and resentment because they've been trying to fight battles alone? I am 100 percent guilty of this "I'm-in-control sin." But in the New Living Testament, Exodus 14:13-14 tells us this: *"Don't be afraid. Just stand still and watch the Lord rescue you today. The Lord himself will fight for you. Just stay calm."* That about sums everything up in this life. Even through the storms, stand still and stay calm because the Lord is in control.

xoxxo

~ N.A. Banda

P.S. One day soon, treat yourself to a pedicure. While you're enjoying your relaxing time, think of Jesus washing your dirty feet. He came to God's children to be a servant and to teach us how to wash the feet of others.

And yes, there will be storms. But my heart longs for others to know Jesus is "all in" for them even through the storms. He longs to make changes in the lives of God's children that lead to a more peaceful and full feeling. Fulfillment. Yes, change is uncomfortable, and sometimes it hurts, but change produces something good in the end, after the race has been run.

For instance, wintertime brings a change in season and many living things — like trees, leaves, fruit, plants, grass, etc. — die, fall off, or sleep to make room for spring's new life, new growth, and new fruit. It's similar with people. God wants His people to die to sin so He can produce a good harvest of Holiness in His creation. Not perfection per se, humans are far from perfect, but in the act of redemption. With redemption and belonging comes a sense of security, meaning, and being loved as part of a much larger family with purpose.

One last thought: Life is short. Eat the dessert, buy the shoes, love and forgive quickly, and serve others. Don't focus on the future. Focus on today and all God has in store for you and you will be filled up.

~ Natalie

DISCUSSION QUESTIONS

If you're reading this book as a Bible study with others, feel free to talk about how it has made an impact. Were there any takeaways? Did any of these stories strike home? Could you relate? If you need discussion questions you might try to thoughtfully answer some of the following, sharing with your group as you feel led.

1. In this present existence, are you willing to be the hands and feet of Jesus in the world? If not, what is holding you back?
2. Are you comfortable sharing the Gospel with friends, family, or strangers? If not, think of some ways you might be able to approach those in the future who don't know God.
3. Do you make time in your day to read a devotional, study God's Word, or talk to God in prayer? If not, how can you make time?
4. When problems arise, do you depend on God for solutions or do you strike out on your own trying to solve problems yourself? In what ways can you learn to depend on God more?
5. Looking back on your life, can you recall any Godcidents or interesting events that might have had God's hand in the works?

6. Are you religiously praying gimee-gimee prayers instead of trying to have a relationship with God?

7. Do you remember a time when God "nailed it" for you? Try to recall details from an event when you knew Jesus was "at the wheel."

8. Romans 8:28 teaches us in a nutshell that God can turn something bad into good. Write your impressions of a time when God did just that. Share your experience with your group if you feel so inclined.

9. When you feel God is asking you to do something for Him, do you follow through or go on about your day? If you don't follow through, what's holding you back from doing more than listening?

10. Praying publicly can be daunting. Is this something you feel comfortable doing? Or are you fearful? Is praying for and with others something you could gradually work on?

11. Jesus didn't promise us that walking in His footsteps would be easy. In fact, He said trials and tribulations will come. Can you share a few scriptures that help you walk the walk?

12. Do you believe that God connects His children? If so, can you share with your group a story of a divine appointment you've

experienced?

13. Sometimes we experience what some have called a "dark night of the soul." Can you relate? If so, has this time made you stronger? In what ways?

14. Jesus said He is the door or the gate to God. Are you willing to surrender all to the Savior? If not, what's holding you back?

15. Do you know someone who is spiritually lost and can't find their way? Is there a reason for not sharing the Gospel with them — perhaps fear is holding you back? Jot down different ways you might approach the lost taking into consideration their religious background or lack thereof.

ABOUT THE AUTHORS

N. A. BANDA considers herself a cool young mom of three girls, (adults now which seems crazy) and wife to an amazing 100% supportive husband who goes by Vic B. A very loud and talkative Puerto Rican nail tech, she was born and reared in the East Bay of Cali, loves food — good food, Pinterest and people. You can find her at coffee shops making friends with complete strangers, loving the beach with Vic and her girls while tanning, and of course Disneyland.

She is thankful for the privilege of planning and being part of Young Lives (along with her eldest daughter who often serves alongside her at summer camp as a nanny), for Thursday Bible study, and for club days filled with food, friends, and fellowship.

Pinterest involved! Her love for decorating has evolved from this social media outlet along with her love for creativity as a nail tech. N.A. started off just like many young moms and she laughed when her youngest daughter graduated high school — amazed she and her husband had successfully raised three humans. "I must say they are all amazing, beautiful, loving young women. It was hard, messy, and worth every minute," she says. Follow N.A. Banda on Instagram: @n.a.banda and Pinterest: Natalie Banda

VICKI H. Moss, contributing editor for Southern Writers Magazine, is a former newspaper columnist, and author of *How to Write for Kids' Magazines; Writing with Voice; Adrift; Smelling Stinkweed;* and *Rogue Hearts.*

With over 500 articles published internationally, she's written for several magazines and was selected to present her fiction and creative nonfiction short stories for three consecutive Southern Women Writers Conferences held at Rome, Georgia's Berry College.

Vicki is also a speaker and serves on faculty at Christian writers conferences. Her stories are frequently published in the *Divine Moments* series by Grace Publishing. For more information about Vicki visit www.

livingwaterfiction.com. Join her on Twitter: vickimoss; Instagram: @vickihmoss; Facebook: Vicki H. Moss, author; and Pinterest: Vicki Moss.

VICKI'S GET LUCKY SOUP RECIPE

INGREDIENTS:

¼ cup butter

1 cup chopped onions or leeks

¾ cup leftover cubed potatoes, cubed

¾ cup leftover sliced or diced carrots , cubed

¼ cup grated celery

5 cups water

½ cup half-and-half

¼ tsp. pepper

Salt to taste

1 cup cooked chicken, shredded

2 Tbsp. chopped fresh chives (or dried chives)

1 (8 oz.) pkg. cream cheese, cubed (If you don't have cream cheese, substitute another cheese, or add ½ cup of half-and-half for a thinner soup without cheese.)

DIRECTIONS:

You may add whatever you have as leftovers from your fridge. This can include roasted carrots or carrots and potatoes left over from a chicken crock pot supper. The grated celery adds a yummy flavor. If you add chicken, shred the meat. Use no more than ½ cup of each veggie if you decide to add veggies other than carrots, potatoes, and celery.

Melt butter in a large pot on medium-high heat. Add onions; cook five minutes or until tender, stirring frequently. (If onions have already been cooked, add them at the end of cooking time and thoroughly heat.)

Add water and half-and-half mixture, then add the carrots and potatoes. If carrots or potatoes are already cooked, wait to add them the last five minutes of cooking time to heat thoroughly.

Bring to boil; cover. Simmer on medium-low heat 20 minutes or until potatoes are tender. Remember to stir occasionally so nothing burns or sticks.

Remove from heat.

With this recipe, you can either puree potatoes to your liking or leave them cubed. If pureed, remove some to puree, then return the potato puree to the stockpot. Cook on medium heat five minutes or until heated through, stirring occasionally.

Add half-and-half and cream cheese or whatever cheese you have on hand; stir. Add chicken. Cook 3-5 minutes or until cheese is melted and mixture blended. Stir in pepper and salt to taste. Sprinkle with chives before serving.

Potato bread goes nicely with Get Lucky Soup. If you have lots of time on your hands, feel free to make your own bread. If not, add potato bread or a different bread to your shopping list. And don't forget to add a simple salad.

Vicki's note: I served my Bible study ladies using fine china and crystal so they would feel special, however, Chinet paper bowls, paper cups, and plasticware work just as well with hardly any cleanup. Just toss and go!

Make your Bible studies a fun time without stress. If that means casual tableware, by all means use paper and plastic. Some of my most fun times with friends have been during outdoor picnics.

I think Jesus would say Amen!

CPSIA information can be obtained
at www.ICGtesting.com
Printed in the USA
BVHW05s1039300718
523023BV00025B/980/P

9 781604 950397